Quick & Easy Way to learn Russian

Alexandra Gordeeva
Saint Petersburg
State University (Russia)

QUALIS BOOKS

ISBN : 81-87838-07-8
ISBN : 9788187838074

1st Published - 2005
4th Printing - 2012
Quick & Easy Way to Learn Russian

Published by
Qualis Books
E-219, IInd Floor, New Rajinder Nagar,
New Delhi - 110 060.
E-mail : qualisbooks@yahoo.co.in

Printed in India at
Kay Kay Printers.
New Delhi.

Quick & Easy Way to Learn Russian

This book is intended for any reader who wishes to learn Russian language & culture in 'Quick & Easy way' just for personal interest as a student, or is about to travel to this beautiful country. As a result the grammar and the vocabulary have been confined to what might be relevant to such a reader so that self-learning process does not become a 'put off' on coming across too much of grammar rules.

Abbreviations used in this book-

m-masculine noun

f-feminine noun

mpl-masculine plural

fpl-feminine plural

In order to facilitate the pronounciation, each word or sentence in Russian is followed by its possible equivalent pronounciation in English.

Good luck!

Contents

Chapter-1

Russian Alphabet

Letter	Pronounced as	Symbol
а	**a** in car; **u** in cut	a/ah
б	**b** in bit	b
в	**v** in vine	v
г	**g** in go	g
д	**d** in do	d
е	**ye** in yet	ye
ё	**yo** in yolk	yo
ж	**s** in measure	zh
з	**z** in zoo	z
и	**ee** in see	ee
й	**y** in boy	y
к	**k** in kiss	k
л	**l** in lady	l
м	**m** in mist	m
н	**n** in not	n
о	**o** in folk	o
п	**p** in pipe	p
р	trilled **r** in rrroll	r
с	**s** in soft	s
т	**t** in tie	t
у	**oo** in root	oo

ф	**f** in farm	f
х	**ch** in Scottish loch	kh
ц	**ts** in lists	ts
ч	**ch** in chapter	ch
ш	**sh** in shut	sh
щ	**sh** in sheep	shch
ь	is used to make the preceding consonant soft	'
ы	**i** in ill	i
ъ	is used to separate two parts of the word	'
э	**e** in net	e
ю	**u** in use	yoo
я	**ya** in yard	ya/yah

Letter Combinations

Letter combination	Pronounced as	Symbol
ай	**igh** in might	igh
яй	**ай**, preceded by the **y** as in yes	yigh
ой	**oy** in toy	oy
ей	**ay** in pay, preceded by a short **y**	yay
уй	**oo** in food followed by **y** as in yes	ooy
юй	**уй**, preceded by a short **y**	yooy

Russian Pronunciation: Vowels

Russian pronunciation rules are rather simple as compared to English. For example, there are no words in Russian that sound the same but have different spelling like English "might" and "mite". By and large, Russian words will sound correctly if you simply read them letter-by-letter.

In general, Russian vowels are divided into two basic types: "soft-indicating" and "hard-indicating" vowels. The "hard-indicating" vowels are **а, э, ы, у, о (a, e, i, oo, o)**. Russian "soft-indicating" vowels are formed from their "hard-indicating" counterparts by adding an English sound of "y" at the beginning. Thus you will get such "soft-indicating" vowels as **я, е, ё, ю, и (ya, ye, yo, yoo, ee)**. Notice, that vowel groups are marked as "soft-indicating" and "hard-indicating" because they indicate whether the following consonant is "hard" or "soft".

Rule #1

In unstressed positions, Russian letter **O** is pronounced like unstressed Russian **A** (вода va-**dah**).

Rule#2

In unstressed positions, Russian letters **Я, Е, Э** (ya, ye, e) are pronounced like a Russian **И** (ee).

Russian	**Pronunciation**
ве-се-ло	**vye**-see-la
яг-**нё**-нок	eeg-**nyo**-nak

Rule #3

The letter Ё is always stressed in Russian words (ёлка - **yo**lka).

Rule #4

To get Russian sound **ы** (i), you should place your tongue in the position right between the positions of English sounds **i** in **kit** and **u** in **sugar**. Then make a new sound of **ы**.

Rule #5

The basic rule to make a "soft-indicating" Russian vowel is to combine a sound of English **y** with corresponding "hard-indicating" vowel. For example, to get Russian **я** you should say **y + a** as if they are one whole (**ya**) (яма - **yah**ma)

Quick reference on "hard-indicating" vowels

Russian letter	Symbol	Pronunciation
А (stressed)	ah	as Ah, but shorter
А (unstressed)	A	as u in but
О (stressed)	o	as aw in law
О (unstressed)	A	as u in but
Ы	i	no English equivalent
У	oo	as oo in wood
Э	e	as e in pet

Consonants

There are 20 consonant letters in the Russian alphabet (**б, в, г, д, ж, з, к, л, м, н, п, р, с, т, ф, х, ц, ч, ш, щ**).

With few exceptions, Russian consonants can be pronounced either "soft" or "hard" depending on the type of a letter that comes after them. For this reason, the 20 consonant letters of the Russian alphabet can designate 37 distinct consonant sounds!

Hard	Soft
moot (m)	**mute (m')**
land (l)	**leap (l')**

Voiced and voiceless consonants

Just like in English, several Russian consonants come in pairs where one letter is pronounced voiced and another one is similar but voiceless. For example, the English letters **b** and **p** make the pair (**bat - pat**). The word "voiced" here means that your vocal chords should vibrate when making a sound.

Voiced-voiceless pairs in the Russian language:

Voiced	Voiceless
б (b)	**п** (p)
в (v)	**ф** (f)
г (g)	**к** (rarely **х**) (kh)
д (d)	**т** (t)
ж (zh)	**ш** (sh)
з (z)	**с** (s)

Rule #1

Russian voiced consonants are pronounced as their voiceless counterparts when they appear in the very end of the word. For instance, the word **год** (year) is actually pronounced as **гот**, the word **глаз** (eye) sounds like **глас**, the word **бог** (god) is said **бох**, etc.

Rule #2

Russian consonants become voiceless when they are followed by other voiceless consonants. For example, the word **подпись** (signature) sounds like **потпись** because the voiced letter **д** is followed by the voiceless **п**.

Classes of Russian pronouns

	1st person	я (yah), мы (mi)	**I, we**
Personal	**2nd person**	ты (ti), вы (vi)	**you (sing), you (plural)**
	3rd person	он (on), она (an**ah**), оно (an**o**), они (an**ee**)	**he, she, it, they**
Reflexive		себя (see**byah**)	**myself, oneself**
Possessive		мой (moy), твой (tvoy),	**my, your (familiar), our,**

	наш (nahsh), ваш (vahsh), свой (svoy)	**your (polite/plural)**
Demonstrative	тот (tot), та, то, те; этот (**e**tat), эта, это; эти; такой (ta**koy**), такая, такое, такие; столько (**stol'**ka)	**that; this; these; such; so much/many**
Interrogative	кто (kto), что (chto), какой (ka**koy**), чей (chey), который (ka**to**riy), сколько (**skol'**ka), насколько (na**skol'**ka)	**who, what, who, what, what/which, whose, which, how much/ many, to what extent**
Indefinite	некто (**nyek**ta), нечто (**nyech**ta), некоторый (**nye**katariy), несколько (**nyes**kal'ka); кто-то (**kto**-ta), кто-нибудь; что-то (**chto**-ta), что-нибудь; какой-то (ka**koy**-ta); кое-кто (**ko**yee-**kto**)	**someone, someone, something, some, some; somebody, something; some; someone**

Relative	кто, что, какой, который, чей, сколько, насколько	**who, what, what/which, which, whose, how much/many, to what extent**
Negative	никто (nee**kto**), ничто (nee**shto**), некого (**nye**kava), нечего (**nye**cheeva), ничей (nee**chey**), нисколько (nee**skol'**ka); никакой (neeka**koy**)	**nobody, nothing, there's nobody to, there's nothing to, nobody's, to no extent**
Determinative	сам (sahm), весь (vyes'), всякий (**vsyah**keey)/каждый (**kahzh**diy), иной (ee**noy**)/другой (droo**goy**), любой (lyoo**boy**)	**oneself, all, everybody, each/every, other/some, another, any**

Noun Gender and Number

There are three genders in Russian: masculine, feminine and neuter. You can usually determine the gender of a noun by its ending. Here are some basic rules, though exceptions exist:

Masculine:

Word	Ending
дом (dom)	in a consonant
чай (chahy)	in-й

Feminine:

Word	Ending
картина (karteena)	in-**a**
семья (syem'yah)	in-**я**

Neuter:

Word	Ending
письмо (pees'mo)	in **-o**
платье (plaht'ye)	in **-e**

Remember that there are no articles in Russian.

Number

English plurals normally end in **-s** or **-es**. In Russian, there are more endings to make plurals. They are all summed up in the table below.

Note: Remove the last letter in a word before adding the new plural ending. If a word ends in a consonant you do not need to remove the last letter.

Noun type	Ending for plural	Example
masculine ending in a hard consonant; feminine ending in **-a**	**-ы**	стол столы рыба рыбы
any nouns ending in **-ь, -й, -я**	**-и**	дверь - двери
masculine and feminine ending in **-k, -г, -х, -ч, -щ, -ж, -ш,**	**-и**	нога ноги лик лики
neuter ending in **-o**	**-a**	окно окна
neuter ending in **-e**	**-я**	море - моря

Some nouns are always singular. These are nouns that designate substances (oxygen, copper), products (cheese, fish), a block of objects (furniture), some actions (hunting, clearing up), feelings (love, health), some vegetables and berries (potato, carrots).

You will have to know the genders and plurals, because they influence the use of adjectives and pronounces. Look at how the word **красивый** (beautiful) changes:

Красивый:

Gender	**Word change**
masculine:	красив<u>ый</u> мяч
feminine:	красив<u>ая</u> девушка
neuter:	красив<u>ое</u> море
plural:	красив<u>ые</u> мячи
all genders)	красив<u>ые</u> девушки
	красив<u>ые</u> моря

Usage of Cases

In Russian, it is the case of a noun that shows what role the noun plays in a sentence. The table below shows how the noun **Алексей** (a male name) changes by cases.

CASES	EXAMPLE SENTENCES	ENGLISH EQUIVALENTS
Nominative	Это Алексей.	This is Alexei.
Genitive	Мы изучаем таблицу Алексея.	We are studying Alexei's chart.
Dative	Ученик дал Алексею таблицу.	A student gave a chart to Alexei.
Accusative	Анна ждёт Алексея.	Ann is waiting for Alexei.
Instrumental	Таблица написана Алексеем.	A chart is written by Alexei.
Prepositional	Друзья говорят об Алексее.	Friends are talking about Alexei.

First, you may see how important case endings are to show the role of a noun. Note, that the contrasting English equivalents have the name Alexei unchanged.

Second, it should be mentioned that the word order does not affect the meaning of a sentence significantly. For example, the sentence **Анна ждёт Алексея** has the same meaning as **Алексея ждёт Анна** as long as you use the accusative of **Алексей**.

The Declension of Singular Nouns

The inflexion of nouns by cases and numbers is called declension (***склонение*** - pronounced as *sklah-**nye**-nee-ye*).

Depending on case endings all singular nouns are divided into three types of declension.

First declension nouns are primarily feminine nouns but there are also several masculine nouns with an initial (dictionary, nominative) form ending in **-а, -я**. For example:

feminine nouns - **трава, земля, химия**
masculine nouns - **папа, дядя, юноша**

First declension nouns end in **-е** in the dative and prepositional cases (**трав**е, **о трав**е). Nouns which have initial form ending in **-ия** (**армия, Наталия**) get the ending **-и** in the dative and prepositional cases (**армии, об армии, Наталии, о Наталии**).

Here is a chart that sums up the endings cf first declension singular nouns.

Cases	Singular nouns endings	Examples *				
Nominative	**-а, -я, -ия**	трава	земля	юноша	химия	Валерия
Genitive	**-ы, -и**	травы	земли	юноши	химии	Валерии
Dative	**-е, -и**	траве	земле	юноше	химии	Валерии
Accusative	**-у, -ю**	траву	землю	юношу	химию	Валерию
Instrumental	**-ой, -ей**	травой	землёй	юношей	химией	Валерией
Prepositional	**-е, -и**	(о) траве	(о) земле	(о) юноше	(о) химии	(о) Валерии

* Stressed vowels are underlined. Endings are in bold.

Second declension nouns nclude:

- masculine nouns with a zero ending in the initial form (стол, олень)
- neuter nouns ending in **-о, е** (неб**о**, пол**е**, поведени**е**)
- nouns ending in -**ий**, -**ие** (гербар**ий**, поведен**ие**)

Second declension nouns in the prepositional case end in **-е** (об олен**е**, о неб**е**, о пол**е**). Masculine nouns with an initial form ending in **-ий** and neuter nouns ending in **-ие** get the ending **-и** in the prepositional case.

The endings typical of second declension singular nouns are summed up in this table.

Cases	Singular nouns endings	Examples *				
Nominative	**zero ending, -о, -е, -ий, -ие**	олень	гербарий	небо	поле	поведение
Genitive	**-а, -я**	оленя	гербария	неба	поля	поведения
Dative	**-у, -ю**	оленю	гербарию	небу	полю	поведению
Accusative	**-я, -о, -е, -ий, -ие**	оленя	гербарий	небо	поле	поведение
Instrumental	**-ем, -ом**	оленем	гербарием	небом	полем	поведением
Prepositional	**-е, -и**	(об) олене	(о) гербарии	(о) небе	(о) поле	(о) поведении

* Stressed vowels are underlined. Endings are in bold.

Third declension nouns are feminine nouns with a zero ending in the initial form (**дочь, сирень, тишь**). Third declension singular nouns in the genitive, dative and prepositional cases end in **-и** (**у сирени, к сирени, о сирени**).

This table sums up the endings of third declension singular nouns.

Case	Singular nouns endings	Examples *	
Nominative	**zero ending**	дочь	сирень
Genitive	**-и**	дочери	сирени
Dative	**-и**	дочери	сирени
Accusative	**zero ending**	дочь	сирень
Instrumental	**-ю**	дочерью	сиренью
Prepositional	**-и**	(о) дочери	(о) сирени

* Stressed vowels are underlined. Endings are in bold.

The Declension of Plural Nouns

There is no strict distinction between declensions of plural nouns in Russian. The charts below sum up the endings for plural nouns and give examples.

First declension

Cases	Plural nouns endings	Examples *	
Nominative	**-ы, -и**	страны	лилии
Genitive	**-й**	стран	лилий
Dative	**-ам, -ям**	странам	лилиям
Accusative	**-ы, -и**	страны	лилии
Instrumental	**-ами, -ями**	странами	лилиями
Prepositional	**-ах, -ях**	(о) странах	(о) лилиях

* Stressed vowels are underlined. Endings are in bold.

Second declension

Cases	Plural nouns endings	Examples *	
Nominative	-а	окна	города
Genitive	-ов	окон	городов
Dative	-ам	окнам	
Accusative	-а	окна	города
Instrumental	-ами	окнами	городами
Prepositional	-ах	(об) окнах	(о) городах

Third declension

Cases	Plural nouns endings	Examples *
Nominative	-и	ладони
Genitive	-й	ладоней
Dative	-ям	ладоням
Accusative	-и	ладони
Instrumental	-ями	ладонями
Prepositional	-ях	(о) ладонях

As you can see from the charts, the nouns of all three

declensions have the same endings in the dative, instrumental and prepositional cases.

In the nominative and accusative cases, the plural nouns may have the endings:

- **-ы/-и** -- typical of nouns of any declension
- **-а/-я** -- typical of second declension nouns only (**берега, озёра, моря**)

Conjugation of Verbs

Changes, which Russian verbs undergo depending on person and number, are called conjugation.

The Present Tense Endings

There are two conjugations in Russian, called the 1st conjugation and the 2nd conjugation (or E-conjugation and И-conjugation, respectively).

The **1st conjugation** verbs are those, which have the letter "**е**" in their endings, for example:

читать (to read)	
я (I)	**читаю**
ты (you - singular)	**читаешь**
он, она, оно (he, she, it)	**читает**
мы (we)	**читаем**
вы (you plural)	**читаете**
они (they)	**читают**

The **2nd conjugation** verbs have the letter "**и**" in their endings.

верить (to believe)

я (I)	**верю**
ты (you - singular)	**веришь**
он, она, оно (he, she, it)	**верит**
мы (we)	**верим**
вы (you - plural)	**верите**
они (they)	**верят**

You will need to determine the conjugation of the verb in order to write correct personal endings. Usually, there is no problem with this for verbs which have stressed endings. For such verbs the same letter is used in writing as in speaking. For example, in words **спишь, гребёшь** the same letter is written as is heard.

Remember:

Conjugation is typical only for present and future tense verbs used in indicative mood. Past tense verbs change only by gender and number.

However if the stress is on the base rather than ending, you will need to determine the conjugation of the verb by looking at its infinitive and applying the following rule.

The **2nd conjugation** verbs (with unstressed ending) are:

1. those, which end in **-ить**, like **заправить, клеить, беспокоить**. Exceptions are: **брить, стелить, побрить, постелить, выстелить**, etc.

2. seven verbs ending in **-еть**: **смотреть, видеть, ненавидеть, зависеть, терпеть, вертеть, обидеть** + all verbs derived from them, like **посмотреть, увидеть, вытерпеть, завертеть, перетерпеть**, etc.

3. four verbs ending in **-ать**: **гнать, дышать, держать, слышать** + all verbs derived from them, like **прогнать, задышать, удержать, расслышать**, etc.

4. The remaining verbs (not mentioned in points 1. to 3.) are **1st conjugation** verbs.

There are some verbs, which can have the endings of both the 1st conjugation and the 2nd conjugation. These are the verbs **хотеть, бежать** and those derived from them (**захотеть, добежать**, etc.).

хотеть (to want)		
	Singular	**Plural**
1st person	хочу	хотим
2nd person	хочешь	хотите
3rd person	хочет	хотят

The Past Tense Endings

The Past Tense of a verb indicates that the action indicated by the verb occurred in the past. The Past Tense ending for both conjugations is -л + gender marker, **-о** for neuter, **-а** for feminine, nothing for masculine in the singular, and **-и** in the plural.

сказать (to say)	
он/я/ты сказал	he(it)/I/you said
она/я/ты сказала	she(it)/I/you said
оно сказало	it said
они/мы/вы сказали	they/we/you said

The Future Tense Endings

Future tense denotes that the action marked by the verb will happen after the moment of speaking.

The simplest and imperfective aspect of a verb can be attained by the use of the verb "быть" (to be). By placing the correct form of "быть" in front of a Russian infinitive, you can create a verb in imperfective future tense. This form of the future tense is called compound.

быть (to be) + читать (to read)	
я буду читать	I shall/will read
ты будешь читать	you (sg.) will read
он/она́/оно́ будет читать	he/she/it will read
мы будем читать	we shall/will read
вы будете читать	you (pl.) will read
они́ будут читать	they will read

Another form of the future tense is called simple. Future simple forms are formed by the verbs of the perfective aspect with the help of prefixes and personal endings.

читать (to read)	
я прочитаю	I shall/will read I shall/will have read
ты прочитаешь	you (sg.) will read you (sg.) will have read
он/она́/оно́ прочитает	he/she/it will read he/she/it will have read
мы прочитаем	we shall/will read we shall/will have read
вы прочитаете	you (pl.) will read you (pl.) will have read
они́ прочитают	they will read they will have read

Proverbs
Пословицы (pasloveetsi)

English	Russian
Actions speak louder than words	Не по словам судят, а по делам
After dinner comes the reckoning	Любишь кататься, люби и саночки возить

All are not hunters that blow the horn	Не всё то золото, что блестит
All bread is not baked in one oven	Не следует всех стричь под одну гребенку
All doors open to courtesy	Ласковое слово не трудно, а споро
All roads lead to Rome	Все дороги ведут в Рим
All that glitters is not gold	Не всё то золото, что блестит.
All things are difficult before they are easy	Лиха беда - начало.
Appetite comes with eating	Аппетит приходит во время еды.
As you make your bed, so must you lie on it	Как постелешь, так и поспишь
Bad workman quarrels with his tools	Плохому танцору и сцена мешает
Before one can say Jack Robinson	Не успеть и глазом моргнуть
Better a little fire to warm us, than a great one to burn us	Хорошего понемножку

Better be born lucky than rich	Не родись красивой, а родись счастливой
Better late than never	Лучше поздно, чем никогда
Calamity is man's true touchstone	Человек познается в беде
Caution is the parent of safety	Береженого и бог бережет
Diligence is the mother of success	Терпенье и труд всё перетрут
Don't look a gift horse in the mouth	Дареному коню в зубы не смотрят
Dot your I's and cross your t's	Поставить все точки над i.
Dumb dogs are dangerous	В тихом омуте черти водятся
Early to bed and early to rise makes a man healthy, wealthy and wise	Кто рано встает, тому Бог дает
East or West - home is best	В гостях хорошо, а дома лучше.
Every dark cloud has a silver lining	Нет худа без добра

Evil chance seldom comes alone	Беда одна не ходит.
Extremes meet	Крайности сходятся.
Faint heart never won fair lady	Смелость города берет.
Far from eye, far from heart	С глаз долой, из сердца вон
First catch your hare	Не дели шкуру неубитого медведя.
Fool's haste is no speed	Поспешишь - людей насмешишь
Four eyes see more than two	Одна голова хорошо, две лучше
Give a fool rope enough, and he will hang himself	Попроси дурака богу молиться, он себе лоб расшибет
Good example is the best sermon	Ничто не убеждает людей лучше примера
Habit cures habit	Клин клином вышибается
Happiness takes no account of time	Счастливые часов не наблюдают
If ifs and ans were pots and pans	Если бы, да кабы во рту росли грибы

If you agree to carry the calf, they'll make you carry the cow	Дай воли на палец - и всю руку откусят
Jack of all trades is master of none	За все браться - ничего не уметь
Let bygones be bygones	Кто старое помянет, тому глаз вон
Let well alone	От добра добра не ищут.
Like begets like	От яблони яблоко, от ели шишка
Make haste slowly	Тише едешь, дальше будешь.
Man proposes but God disposes	Человек предполагает, а бог располагает
Neck or nothing	Либо пан, либо пропал.
No garden without its weeds	Нет худа без добра
One good turn deserves another	Долг платежом красен
One man's meat is another man's poison	Каждому свое

Plenty is no plague	Каши маслом не испортишь
Put not your hand between the bark and the tree	Не суй носа в чужое просо
Rain at seven, fine at eleven	Семь пятниц на неделе
Rome was not built in a day	Не сразу Москва строилась.
Small rain lays great dust	Мал золотник, да дорог
Stolen pleasures are sweetest	Запретный плод сладок, а человек падок
The cap fits	Не в бровь, а в глаз
The Dutch have taken Holland!	Америку открыл!
The game is not worth the candle	Овчинка выделки не стоит
The more the merrier	В тесноте, да не в обиде
Truth comes out of the mouths of babes and sucklings	Устами младенца глаголит истина.
Wash your dirty linen at home	Не выноси сора из избы

We know not what is good until we have lost it	Что имеем, не храним, потерявши, плачем
What is bred in the bone will not go out of the flesh	Горбатого могила исправит
What must be, must be	Чему быть, того не миновать
Wise man changes his mind, a fool never will	Хоть кол на голове теши, а он всё свое
Word spoken is past recalling	Слово - не воробей, вылетит - не поймаешь
You made your bed, now lie in it	Сам заварил кашу, сам и расхлебывай
Zeal without knowledge is a runaway horse	Рвенье без ученья - не польза, а беда

Chapter-2

Parts of the Body

Части тела (chahstee tyela)

English	Russian	Pronunciation
Abdomen	живот (m)	zhi-**vot**
Ankle	лодыжка (f)	la-**dish**-ka
Appendix	аппендикс (m)	ap-**pyen**-deeks
Arm	рука (f)	roo-**kah**
Armpit	подмышка (f)	pad-**mish**-ka
Back	спина (f)	spee-**nah**
Beard	борода (f)	ba-ra-**dah**
Belly	живот (m)	zhi-**vot**
Bladder	пузырь (m)	poo-**zir'**
Blood	кровь (f)	krof'
Body	тело (n)	**tye**-la
Bone	кость (f)	kost'
Bosom	грудь (f)	groot'

English	Russian	Pronunciation
Brain	мозг (m)	mosk
Breast	грудь (f)	groot'
Cheek	щека (f)	shchee-**kah**
Chest	грудная клетка (f)	grood-**nah-**ya **klyet**-ka
Chin	подбородок (m)	pad-ba-**ro-**dak
Collarbone	ключица (f)	klyoo-**chee-**tsa
Diaphragm	диафрагма (f)	dee-af-**rahg**-ma
Diastole	диастола (f)	dee-**ahs**-ta-la
Ear	ухо (n)	**oo-**kha
Elbow	локоть (m)	**lo-**kat'
Eye	глаз (m)	glahs
Eyeball	глазное яблоко (n)	glaz-**no-**ye **yahb**-la-ka
Eyebrow	бровь (f)	brof'
Eyelash	ресницы (pl)	rees-**nee-**tsi
Eyelid	веко (n)	**vye-**ka
Face	лицо (n)	lee-**tso**
Finger	палец (m)	**pah-**leets
Fist	кулак (m)	koo-**lahk**
Flesh	плоть (f)	plot'

English	Russian	Pronunciation
Foot	ступня (f)	stoop-**nyah**
Forehead	лоб (m)	lop
Gall-bladder	желчный пузырь (m)	**zhelch**-niy poo-**zir'**
Gum	десна (f)	dees-**nah**
Hair	волосы (pl)	**vo**-la-si
Hand	рука (f)	roo-**kah**
Head	голова (f)	ga-la-**vah**
Heart	сердце (n)	**syer**-tse
Heel	пятка (f)	**pyaht**-ka
Hip	бедро (n)	beed-**ro**
Intestine	кишечник (m)	kee-**shech**-neek
Joint	сустав (m)	soos-**tahf**
Knee	колено (n)	ka-**lye**-na
Kidney	почка (f)	**poch**-ka
Large intestine	толстая кишка (f)	**tol**-sta-ya keesh-**kah**
Leg	нога (f)	na-**gah**
Lip	губа (f)	goo-**bah**
Liver	печень (f)	**pye**-cheen'

English	Russian	Pronunciation
Lung	легкое (n)	**lyokh**-ka-ye
Moustache	усы (pl)	oo-**si**
Mouth	рот (m)	rot
Muscle	мышца (f)	**mish**-tsa
Nail	ноготь (m)	**no**-gat'
Neck	шея (f)	**she**-ya
Nerve	нерв (m)	nyerf
Nose	нос (m)	nos
Palm	ладонь (f)	la-**don'**
Penis	пенис (m)	**pye**-nees
Rib	ребро (n)	reeb-**ro**
Shoulder	плечо (m)	plee-**cho**
Sinus	пазуха (f)	**pah**-zoo-kha
Skin	кожа (f)	**ko**-zha
Skull	череп (m)	**che**-reep
Small intestine	малая кишка (f)	**mah**-la-ya keesh-**kah**
Sole	ступня (f)	stoop-**nyah**
Spine	позвоночник (m)	paz-va-**noch**-neek

English	Russian	Pronunciation
Stomach	желудок (m)	zhi-**loo**-dak
Systole	систола (f)	**sees**-ta-la
Temple	висок (m)	vee-**sok**
Thigh	бедро (n)	beed-**ro**
Throat	горло (n)	**gor**-la
Thumb	большой палец (m)	bal'-**shoy pah**-leets
Toe	палец (m)	**pah**-leets
Tongue	язык (m)	ya-**zik**
Tooth	зуб (m)	zoop
Vein	вена (f)	**vye**-na
Vertebra	позвонок (m)	paz-va-**nok**
Waist	талия (f)	**tah**-lee-ya
Wrist	запястье (n)	za-**pyahst'**-ye

Chapter-3

Climate
Климат (<u>klee</u>mat)

cold холодно (**kho**-lad-na)
It will be (very) cold tomorrow.
Завтра будет (очень) холодно.
Zahf-tra **boo-**deet (**o-**cheen') **kho-**lad-na.

hot жарко (**zhahr**-ka)
It was (very) hot last night.
Прошлой ночью было (очень) жарко.
Prosh-lay **noch'-**yoo **bi**-la (**o-**cheen') **zhahr-**ka.

good/bad weather хорошая/плохая погода (kha-**ro**-sha-ya/pla-**khah**-ya pa-**go**-da)
The weather is going to be bad.
Наступает плохая погода.
Nas-too-**pah-**yeet pla-**khah-**ya pa-**go-**da.

The weather is very fine.
Погода очень хорошая.
Pa-**go-**da **o-**cheen' kha-**ro-**sha-ya.

What will the weather be like tomorrow?
Какая завтра погода?
Ka-**kah-**ya **zahf-**tra pa-**go-**da?

sunny солнечно (**sol**-neech-na), sun солнце (**son**-tse)
The sun is not shining.
Солнце не светит.
Son-tse nye **svye-**teet.

cool прохладно (prakh-**lahd**-na)
It is cool today.
Сегодня прохладно.
See-**vod-**nya prakh-**lahd-**na.

It is pleasantly warm today.
Сегодня тепло.
See-**vod-**nya teep-**lo**.

From sunrise to sunset
От рассвета до заката
Ot ras-**vye-**ta do za-**kah-**ta

In the sunshine
На солнце
Na **son-**tse

What is the temperature (today)?
Сколько (сегодня) градусов?
Skol'-ka (see-**vod-**nya) **grah-**doo-saf?

The temperature is five degrees below zero (today).
(Сегодня) пять градусов ниже нуля.
(See-**vod-**nya) pyaht' **grah**-doo-saf **nee-**zhe noo-**lyah**.

What is the weather forecast?
Какой прогноза погоды?
Ka-**koy** prag-**nos** pa-**go**-di?

What are the weather conditions of Moscow?
Каковы погодные условия Москвы?
Ka-ka-**vi** pa-**god**-ni-ye oos-**lo**-vee-ya Mas-**kvi**?

It is windy today.
Сегодня ветрено.
See-**vod**-nya **vye**-tree-na.

Chapter-4

Animals

Животные (zhivotniyee)

English	Russian	Pronunciation
Animal	животное (n)	zhi-**vot**-na-ye
Bull	бык	bik
Bullock	вол	vol
Buffalo	буйвол	**booy**-val
Bitch	сука	**soo**-ka
Calf	теленок	tee-**lyo**-nak
Cat	кот (m), кошка (f)	kot (m), **kosh**-ka (f)
Chameleon	хамелеон	kha-mee-lee-**on**
Camel	верблюд	veer-**blyoot**
Cow	корова	ka-**ro**-va
Dangerous	опасный (m),	a-**pahs**-niy (m),
	опасная (f)	a-**pahs**-na-ya (f)
Deer	олень (m), лань (f)	a-**lyen'** (m), lahn' (f)
Dog	собака (f)	sa-**bah**-ka

English	Russian	Pronunciation
Donkey	осёл (m), ослица (f)	a-**syol** (m), as-**lee**-tsa (f)
Elephant	слон (m), слониха (f)	slon (m), sla-**nee**-kha (f)
Endangered	в опасности	va-**pahs**-nas-tee
Fox	лиса (f)	lee-**sah**
Goat	козел (m), коза (f)	ka-**zyol** (m), ka-**zah** (f)
Hare	заяц	**zah**-yats
Heifer	телка	**tyol**-ka
Horse	конь (m), лошадь (f)	kon' (m), **lo**-shat' (f)
Hound	охотничья собака (f)	a-**khot**-neech-ya sa-**bah**-ka
Indian Elephant	индийский слон	een-**deey**-skeey slon
Jackal	шакал	sha-**kahl**
Lamb	ягненок	yeeg-**nyo**-nak
Leopard	леопард	lee-a-**pahrt**
Lion	лев	lyef

English	Russian	Pronunciation
Mare	кобыла	ka-**bi**-la
Mongoose	мангуст	man-**goost**
Monkey	обезьяна (f)	a-beez'-**yah**-na
Mouse	мышь (f)	mish
Mule	мул	mool
Pig	свинья (f)	sveen'-**yah**
Pup	щенок	shchee-**nok**
Python	питон (m)	pee-**ton**
Ram	баран	ba-**rahn**
Rhinoceros	носорог	na-sa-**rok**
Sheep	овца (f), баран (m)	af-**tsah** (f), ba-**rahn** (m)
Skunk	скунс	skoons
Snake	змея (f)	zmee-**yah**
Squirrel	белка (f)	**byel**-ka
Stag	олень	a-**lyen'**
Swine	поросенок (m)	pa-ra-**syo**-nak
Tiger	тигр	teegr
Tom	самец	sa-**myets**

English	Russian	Pronunciation
Wolf	волк	volk
Crab	краб (m)	krahp
Crocodile	крокодил (m)	kra-ka-**deel**
Fish	рыба (f)	**ri**-ba
Leech	пиявка (f)	pee-**yahf**-ka
Tortoise	черепаха (f)	chee-ree-**pah**-kha

Chapter-5

Birds

Птицы (pteetsi)

English	Russian	Pronunciation
Bat	летучая мышь (f)	lee-**too**-cha-ya mish
Bird	птица (f)	**ptee**-tsa
Cock	петух (m)	pee-**tookh**
Crane	журавль (m),	zhoo-**rahvl'** (m),
	цапля (f)	**tsahp**-lya (f)
Crow	ворона (f),	va-**ro**-na (f),
	ворон (m)	**vo**-ran (m)
Cuckoo	кукушка (f)	koo-**koosh**-ka
Dove	голубь (m)	**go**-loop'
Duck	утка (f)	**oot**-ka
Hen	курица (f)	**koo**-ree-tsa
Kite	сокол (m),	**so**-kal (m),
	ястреб (m)	**yahs**-treep (m)
Nightingale	соловей (m)	sa-la-**vyey**

English	Russian	Pronunciation
Owl	сова (f)	sa-**vah**
Parrot	попугай (m)	pa-poo-**gahy**
Partridge	куропатка (f)	koo-ra-**paht**-ka
Peacock	павлин (m)	pav-**leen**
Pigeon	голубь (m)	**go**-loop'
Sparrow	воробей (m)	va-ra-**byey**
Swan	лебедь (m)	**lye**-beet'
Vulture	гриф (m)	greef

Chapter-6

Insects and Crawlers

Насекомые и пресмыкающееся

(naseekomiyee ee preesmikahyooshcheeyeesya)

English	Russian	Pronunciation
Ant	муравей (m)	moo-ra-**vyey**
Bee	пчела (f)	pchee-**lah**
Bug	клоп (m)	klop
Butterfly	бабочка (f)	**bah**-bach-ka
Fly	муха (f)	**moo**-kha
Frog	лягушка (f)	lya-**goosh**-ka
Germ	зародыш (m)	za-**ro**-dish
Glow-worm	жук-светляк (m)	**zhook**sveet-**lyahk**
Insect	насекомое (n)	na-see-**ko**-ma-ye
Lizard	ящерица (f)	**yah**-shchee-ree-tsa
Locust	саранча (f)	sa-ran-**chah**
Mosquito	комар (m)	ka-**mahr**
Scorpion	скорпион (m)	skar-pee-**on**
Spider	паук (m)	pa-**ook**
Snail	улитка (f)	oo-**leet**-ka
Wasp	оса (f)	a-**sah**

Chapter-7

Plants and Flowers
Цветы и Растения
(tsveeti ee rastyeneeya)

English	Russian	Pronunciation
Acacia	акация (f)	a-**kah**-tsi-ya
Balsam	бальзамин (m)	bal'-za-**meen**
Camomile	ромашка (f)	ra-**mahsh**-ka
Chrysanthemum	хризантема (f)	khree-zan-**te**-ma
Daisy	маргаритка (f)	mar-ga-**reet**-ka
Gladiolus	гладиолус (m)	gla-dee-**o**-loos
Indian Hemp	индийская конопля (f)	een-**deey**-ska-ya ka-nap-**lyah**
Jasmine	жасмин (m)	zhas-**meen**
Lilac	сирень (f)	see-**ryen'**
Lily	лилия (f)	**lee**-lee-ya
Lotus	лотос (m)	**lo**-tas
Magnolia	магнолия (f)	mag-**no**-lee-ya
Marigold	ноготки (pl)	na-gat-**kee**
Mushroom	гриб (m)	greep
Myrtle	мирт (m)	meert
Narcissus	нарцисс (m)	nar-**tsis**
Rose	роза (f)	**ro**-za

Chapter-8

House and House-Hold Articles
Дом и домашние предметы
(dom ee da<u>mahsh</u>neeyee preed<u>mye</u>ti)

English	Russian	Pronunciation
Abattoir	скотобойня (f)	ska-ta-**boy**-nya
Ante-chamber	прихожая (f)	pree-**kho**-zha-ya
Apartment house	многоквартирный дом (m)	**mno**-ga-kvar-**teer**-niy dom
Arch	арка (f)	**ahr**-ka
Armchair	кресло (n)	**kryes**-la
Attic	мансарда (f), чердак (m)	man-**sahr**-da (f), cheer-**dahk** (m)
Air freshener	освежитель воздуха (m)	as-vee-**zhi**-teel' **voz**-doo-kha
Ashtray	пепельница (f)	**pye**-peel'-nee-tsa
Balcony	балкон (m)	bal-**kon**
Barrack	барак (m)	ba-**rahk**
Beam	перекладина (f)	pee-reek-**lah**-dee-na

English	Russian	Pronunciation
Basket	корзина (f)	kar-**zee**-na
Bathmat	банный коврик (m)	**bahn**-niy **kov**-reek
Bathroom	ванная (комната) (f)	**vahn**-na-ya **kom**-na-ta
Bath-salts	банные соли (pl)	**bahn**-ni-yee **so**-lee
Bath-sheet	банная простынь (f)	**bahn**-na-ya **pros**-tin'
Bath-towel	махровое полотенце (n)	makh-**ro**-va-ye pa-la-**tyen**-tse
Bathtub	ванна (f)	**vahn**-na
Battlements	зубчатая стена (f)	**zoop**-cha-ta-ya stee-**nah**
Bed	кровать (f)	kra-**vaht'**
Bedroom	спальня (f)	**spahl'**-nya
Bedsheet	простыня (f)	pras-ti-**nyah**
Bedspread	покрывало (n)	pak-ri-**vah**-la
Bench	скамья (f)	skam'-**yah**
Blanket	одеяло (n)	a-dee-**yah**-la
Bolster	подушка (f), валик (m)	pa-**doosh**-ka (f), **vah**-leek (m)
Bottle	бутылка (f)	boo-**til**-ka
Bottle opener	открывалка (f)	at-kri-**vahl**-ka

English	Russian	Pronunciation
Bowl	чаша, миска (f)	**chah**-sha, **mees**-ka
Box	коробка (f)	ka-**rop**-ka
Bracket	держатель (m)	deer-**zhah**-teel'
Brick	кирпич (m)	keer-**peech**
Broom	метла (f)	meet-**lah**
Brush	щетка (f)	**shchyot**-ka
Bucket	ведро (n)	veed-**ro**
Building	здание (n)	**zdah**-nee-ye
Bungalow	бунгало (n)	boon-**ga**-la
Cabinet	кабинет (m)	ka-bee-**nyet**
Candle	свеча (f)	svee-**chah**
Candlestick	подсвечник (m)	pat-**svyesh**-neek
Canister	канистра (f)	ka-**nees**-tra
Carpet	ковер (m)	ka-**vyor**
Can opener	консервный нож (m)	kan-**syerv**-niy nosh
Carpet tile	половая плитка (f)	pa-la-**vah**-ya **pleet**-ka
Casket	шкатулка (f)	shka-**tool**-ka
Ceiling	потолок (m)	pa-ta-**lok**
Censer	курильница (f)	koo-**reel'**-nee-tsa

English	Russian	Pronunciation
Chair	стул (m)	stool
Chandelier	люстра (f)	**lyoos**-tra
Chimney	труба (f)	troo-**bah**
Chopping-board	разделочный стол (m)	raz-**dye**-lach -niy stol
Churner	сбивалка (f)	sbee-**vahl**-ka
Cigarette Lighter	сигарета (f) зажигалка (f)	see-ga-**rye**-ta za-zhi-**gahl**-ka
Cloister	монастырь (m)	ma-nas-**tir'**
Closet	чулан (m)	choo-**lahn**
Closet-(for clothes)	шкаф (m)	shkahf
Clothes-basket	бельевая корзина (f)	beel'-yee-**vah**-ya kar-**zee**-na
Clothes-brush	платяная щетка (f)	pla-tya-**nah**-ya **shchot**-ka
Clothes-drier	сушилка (f)	soo-**shil**-ka
Clothes-hanger	вешалка (f)	**vye**-shal-ka
Clothes-line	веревка для сушки белья (f)	vee-**ryof**-ka dlya **soosh**-kee beel'-**yah**
Clothes-moth	моль (f)	mol'

English	Russian	Pronunciation
Clothes peg	прищепка (f)	pree-**shchep**-ka
Clothes rack	вешалка (f)	**vye**-shal-ka
Compact isk	компактный диск (m)	kam-**pahkt**-niy deesk
Computer	компьютер (m)	kamp'-**yoo**-ter
Corkscrew	штопор (m)	**shto**-par
Corridor	коридор (m)	ka-ree-**dor**
Cottage	коттедж (m)	ka-**tetsh**
Couch	диван, кушетка (f)	dee-**vahn**, koo-**shet**-ka
Courtyard	двор (m)	dvor
Cup	чашка (f)	**chahsh**-ka
Cupboard (on wall)	сервант (m), шкаф (m)	seer-**vahnt**
Curtain	занавеска (f)	za-na-**vyes**-ka
Cushion	подушка (f)	pa-**doosh**-ka
Cutlery	ножевые изделия (pl.)	na-zhi-**vi**-ye eez-**dye**-lee-ya
Dias	гостиная (f)	gas-**tee**-na-ya
Dinning-hall	столовая (f)	sta-**lo**-va-ya
Dinning-room	столовая (f)	sta-**lo**-va-ya
Dinning-table	обеденный	a-**bye**-deen-niy stol

English	Russian	Pronunciation
	стол (m)	
Dinning-knife	обеденный нож (m)	a-**bye**-deen-niy nosh
Dinning-plate	обеденная	a-**bye**-deen-na-ya
	тарелка (f)	ta-**ryel**-ka
Dinning-trolley	обеденный	a-**bye**-deen-niy
	столик (m)	**sto**-leek
Dishwasher	посудомоечная	pa-**soo**-da-**mo**-eesh
	машина (f)	-na-ya ma-**shi**-na
Door	дверь (m)	dvyer'
Doorbell	дверной звонок (m)	dveer-**noy** zva-**nok**
Doorchain	дверная цепь (f)	dveer-**nah**-ya tsep'
Doorframe	дверная коробка (f)	dveer-**nah**-ya ka-**rop**-ka
Doorstep	порог (m)	pa-**rok**
Drain	канализация (f)	ka-na-lee-**zah**-tsi-ya
Drawer	ящик (m)	**yah**-shcheek
Drawing room	гостиная (f)	gas-**tee**-na-ya
Dressing table	туалетный	too-a-**lyet**-niy
	столик (m)	**sto**-leek
Eaves	карниз (m)	kar-**nees**
Fan	вентилятор (m)	veen-tee-**lyah**-tar
Finger bowl	чаша для омовения	**chah**-sha dlya a-ma-

English	Russian	Pronunciation
	пальцев (f)	**vye**-nee-ya **pahl'**-tsef
Floor	пол (m)	pol
Fork	вилка (f)	**veel**-ka
Foundation	фундамент (m)	foon-**dah**-meent
Frying pan	сковорода (f)	ska-va-ra-**dah**
Funnel	дымоход (m)	di-ma-**khot**
Gallery	галерея (f)	ga-lee-**rye**-ya
Gas-cooker	газовая плитка (f)	**gah**-za-va-ya **pleet**-ka
Gas-cylinder	газовый баллон (m)	**gah**-za-viy ba-**lon**
Glass	стакан (m)	sta-**kahn**
Grate	жаровня (f),	zha-**rov**-nya (f),
	камин (m)	ka-**meen** (m)
Hall	зал (m)	zahl
Hand wash	рукомойник (m)	roo-ka-**moy**-neek
Hearth	дом, камин (m)	dom, ka-**meen**
House	дом (m)	dom
Inkpot	чернильница (f)	cheer-**neel'**-nee-tsa
Jar	банка (f)	**bahn**-ka
Jug	кувшин (m)	koof-**shin**
Key	ключ (m)	klyooch
Kitchen	кухня (f)	**kookh**-nya

English	Russian	Pronunciation
Knife	нож (m)	nosh
Knife (folding)	складной нож (m)	sklad-**noy** nosh
Knife and fork	еда (f)	yee-**dah**
Ladle	ковш (m)	kofsh
Lamp	лампа (f)	**lahm**-pa
Lid	крышка (f)	**kri**-sha
Lock	замок (m)	za-**mok**
Mat	коврик (m)	**kov**-reek
Match	спичка (f)	**speech**-ka
Mattress	матрац (m)	mat-**rahs**
Medicine cabinet	медицинский кабинет (m)	mee-dee-**tsin**-skeey ka-bee-**nyet**
Microwave oven	микроволновая печь (f)	meek-ra-val-**no**-va-ya pyech
Mug	кружка (f)	**kroosh**-ka
Mug (beer)	пивная кружка (f)	peev-**nah**-ya **kroosh**-ka
Needle	игла (f)	eeg-**lah**
Niche	ниша (f)	**nee**-sha
Oven	духовка (f)	doo-**khof**-ka
Peel	кожа, шелуха (f)	**ko**-zha, shi-loo-**khah**
Peephole	глазок (m)	gla-**zok**

English	Russian	Pronunciation
Peg	затычка (f)	za-**tich**-ka
Plaster	пластырь (m)	**plahs**-tir'
Plate	тарелка (f)	ta-**ryel**-ka
Plinth	плинтус (m)	**pleen**-toos
Portico	портик (m)	**por**-teek
Quilt	стеганое	**styo**-ga-na-ye
	одеяло (n)	a-dee-**yah**-la
Radio	радио (n)	**rah**-dee-a
Rafter	стропило (n)	stra-**pee**-la
Railing	ограда (f)	ag-**rah**-da
Recordplayer	проигрыватель (m)	pra-**eeg**-ri-va-teel'
Refrigerator	холодильник (m)	kha-la-**deel'**-neek
Rocking-chair	кресло-качалка (n)	**kryes**-laka-**chahl**-ka
Roof	крыша (f)	**kri**-sha
Room	комната (f)	**kom**-na-ta
Rope	веревка (f),	vee-**ryof**-ka (f),
	канат (m)	ka-**naht** (m)
Sack	мешок (m)	mee-**shok**
Safe	сейф (m)	syeyf
Saucepan	кастрюля (f)	kas-**tryoo**-lya
Shed	сарай (m)	sa-**rahy**

English	Russian	Pronunciation
Shower	душ (m)	doosh
Sieve	сито (n)	**see**-ta
Sink (kitchen)	раковина (f)	**rah**-ka-vee-na
Sofa	софа (f)	sa-**fah**
Sofa-bed	диван-кровать (m)	dee-**vahn**kra-**vaht'**
Spittoon	плевательница (f)	plee-**vah**-teel'-nee-tsa
Spoon	ложка (f)	**losh**-ka
Stair	лестница (f)	**lyes**-nee-tsa
Steeple	башня (f)	**bahsh**-nya
Stick	прут (m)	proot
Stone	камень (m)	**kah**-meen'
Stool	табурет (m)	ta-boo-**ryet**
Storey	этаж (m)	ee-**tahsh**
Stove	печь (f)	pyech
String	шнурок (m)	shnoo-**rok**
Studio apartment	квартира-студия (f)	kvar-**tee**-ra
Table	стол (m)	stol
Table cloth	скатерть (f)	**skah**-teert'
Tape-recorder	магнитофон (m)	mag-nee-ta-**fon**
Teacloth	чайная скатерть/ салфетка (f)	**chahy**-na-ya **skah**-teert' / sal-**fyet**-ka

English	Russian	Pronunciation
Tea-cosy	чехольчик (на чайник) (m)	chee-**khol'**-cheek (na **chahy**-neek)
Teacup	чашка (f)	**chahsh**-ka
Teakettle	чайник (m)	**chahy**-neek
Television	телевизор (m)	tee-lee-**vee**-zar
Thimble	наперсток (m)	na-**pyors**-tak
Tile	плитка (f)	**pleet**-ka
Tissue paper	салфетка (f)	sal-**fyet**-ka
Toaster	тостер (m)	**tos**-ter
Tongs	щипцы (pl.)	shcheep-**tsi**
Torch	фонарь (m)	fa-**nahr'**
Tray	поднос (m)	pad-**nos**
Tumbler	тумблер (m)	**toomb**-leer
Umbrella	зонт (m)	zont
Urinal	ночной горшок (m)	nach-**noy** gar-**shok**
Vase	ваза (f)	**vah**-za
Wall	стена (f)	stee-**nah**
Wall-painting	фреска (f)	**fryes**-ka
Washing-machine	стиральная машина (f)	stee-**rahl'**-na-ya ma-**shee**-na
Washing-powder	стиральный	stee-**rahl'**-niy

English	Russian	Pronunciation
	порошок (m)	pa-ra-**shok**
Whitewash	побелка (f)	pa-**byel**-ka
Wick	фитиль (m)	**fee**-teel'
Window	окно (n)	ak-**no**

Chapter-9

Toiletries

Туалетные принадлежности

(too'alyetniye preenadlyezhnastee)

English	Russian	Pronunciation
Brush	щетка (f)	**shchyot**-ka
Dandruff shampoo	шампунь от перхоти (m)	sham-**poon'** at **pyer**-kha-tee
Deodorant	дезодорант (m)	dee-za-da-**rahnt**
Mouth-wash	полоскание (n)	pa-las-**kah**-nee-ye
Perfume	духи (pl.)	doo-**khee**
Razor	бритва (f)	**breet**-va
Razor (electric)	бритва (электрическая) (f)	**breet**-va (ee-leek-**tree**-chees-ka-ya)
Roll-on deodorant	шариковый дезодорант (m)	**shah**-ree-ka-viy dee-za-da-**rahnt**
Scissors	ножницы (pl.)	**nozh**-nee-tsi
Shampoo	шампунь (m)	sham-**poon'**

English	Russian	Pronunciation
Shaving brush	кисточка для бритья (f)	**kees**-tach-ka dlya breet'-**yah**
Shaving cream	крем для бритья (m)	kryem dlya breet'-**yah**
Soap	мыло (n)	**mi**-la
Sunblock	солнцезащитный крем (m)	**son**-tse-za-**shchit**-niy kryem
Suntan lotion	лосьон для загара (m)	las'-**yon** dlya za-**gah**-rah
Tissue paper	салфетка (f)	sal-**fyet**-ka
Toothbrush	зубная щетка (f)	zoob-**nah**-ya **shchyot**-ka
Toothpaste	зубная паста (f)	zoob-**nah**-ya **pahs**-ta
Tooth powder	зубной порошок (m)	zoob-**noy** pa-ra-**shok**
Towel	полотенце (n)	pa-la-**tyen**-tse
Underpants	кальсоны (pl.), трусы (pl.)	kal'-**so**-ni, troo-**si**
Undergarments	нижнее белье (n)	**neezh**-nee-ye beel'-**yo**

Chapter-10

School
Школа (<u>shko</u>la)

I am studying business.
Я изучаю бизнес.
Yah ee-zoo-**chah-**yoo **beez**-nes.

I am studying at college.
Я учусь в колледже.
Yah oo-**choos'** f **ko**-leed-zhe.

What grade are you in?
В каком ты классе?
F ka-**kom** ti **klahs**-sye?

What do you do after school?
Что ты делаешь после школы?
Shto ti **dye**-la-eesh **pos**-lee **shko**-li?

Is there a creche here?
Здесь есть ясли?
Zdyes' yest' **yahs**-lee?

Where is the playground?
Где (находится) детская площадка?
Gdye (na-**kho**-deet-sya) **dyet**-ska-ya pla-**shchaht**-ka?

Are there swings in the school?
В школе есть качели?
F **shko**-lye yest' ka-**che**-lee?

And a slide too?
И каток тоже?
I ka-**tok to**-zhe?

Chapter-11

Clothing

Одежда (adyezhda)

English	Russian	Pronunciation
Apron	передник (m),	pee-**ryed**-neek (m),
	фартук (m)	**fahr**-took (m)
Bathing-cap	купальная	koo-**pahl'**-na-ya
	шапочка (f)	**shah**-pach-ka
Bathing-suit	купальник (m)	koo-**pahl'**-neek
Bathrobe	купальный	
	халат (m)	koo-**pahl'**-niy kha-**laht**
Belt	пояс (m)	**po**-yas
Bikini	бикини (n)	bee-**kee**-nee
Blanket	одеяло (n)	a-dee-**yah**-la
Blouse	блузка (f)	**bloos**-ka
Blue jeans	джинсы (pl.)	**dzhin**-tsi
Bodice	корсаж (m)	kar-**sahzh**

English	Russian	Pronunciation
Boots	бутсы (pl.)	**boot**-si
Border	кайма (f)	kay-**mah**
Bra	бюстгальтер (m)	byooz-**gahl**-teer
Brocade	парча (f)	par-**chah**
Button	пуговица (f)	**poo**-ga-vee-tsa
Canvas	канва (f)	kan-**vah**
Cap	кепка (f)	**kyep**-ka
Cardigan	кардиган (m)	kar-dee-**gahn**
Cashmere	кашемир (m)	ka-shee-**meer**
Chintz	ситец (m)	**see**-teets
Cloak	плащ (m), мантия (f)	plahshch (m), **mahn**-tee-ya (f)
Cloth	ткань (f)	tkahn'
Coat	пальто (n)	pal'-**to**
Corduroy	вельвет (m)	veel'-**vyet**
Corduroys	вельветовые брюки (pl.)	veel'-**vye**-ta-vi-ye **bryoo**-kee

English	Russian	Pronunciation
Corset	корсет (m)	kar-**syet**
Damask	дамаст (m)	da-**mahst**
Darning	штопка (f)	**shtop**-ka
Dress	платье (n)	**plaht'**-ye
Dressing-gown	платье (n)	**plaht'**-ye
Flannel	фланель (f)	fla-**nel'**
Gloves	перчатки (pl.)	peer-**chaht**-kee
Handkerchief	носовой платок (m)	na-sa-**voy** pla-**tok**
Hat	шляпа (f), шапка (f)	**shlyah**-pa (f), **shahp**-ka (f)
Jacket	куртка (f)	**koort**-ka
Jersey	вязаная одежда (f)	**vyah**-za-na-ya a-**dyezh**-da
Knitted	вязаный, трикотажный	**vyah**-za-niy, tree-ka-**tahzh**-niy

English	Russian	Pronunciation
Lace	кружево (n)	**kroo**-zhee-va
Leather-	кожаная	**ko**-zha-na-ya
jacket	куртка (f)	**koort**-ka
Lingerie	дамское	**dahms**-ka-ye
	белье (n)	beel'-**yo**
Lining	подкладка (f)	pat-**klaht**-ka
Muffler	теплый	
	шарф (m)	**tyop**-liy shahrf
Napkin	салфетка (f)	sal-**fyet**-ka
Nightgown	ночная	nach-**nah**-ya
	рубашка (f)	roo-**bahsh**-ka
Pajamas	пижама (f)	pee-**zhah**-ma
Pants	брюки (pl.)	**bryoo**-kee
Panties	шорты (pl.)	**shor**-ti
Parka	парка (f)	**pahr**-ka
Petticoat	нижняя юбка (f)	**neezh**-nya-ya **yoop**-ka
Pocket	карман (m)	kar-**mahn**

English	Russian	Pronunciation
Polyester	полиэстер (m)	pa-lee-es-**ter**
Raincoat	непромокаемое пальто (n)	nee-pra-ma-**kah**-ee-ma-ye pal'-**to**
Sackcloth	машковина (f)	mash-ka-**vee**-na
Scarf	платок (m)	pla-**tok**
Serge	серж (m), саржа (f)	syersh (m), **sahr**-zha (f)
Shawl	шаль (f)	shahl'
Shirt	рубашка (f)	roo-**bahsh**-ka
Skirt	юбка (f)	**yoop**-ka
Sleeve	рукав (m)	roo-**kahf**
Slip	нижняя юбка (f)	**neezh**-nya-ya **yoop**-ka
Sportswear	спортивная одежда (f)	spar-**teev**-na-ya a-**dyezh**-da
Stitching	подшивание (n)	pat-shee-**vah**-nee-ye

English	Russian	Pronunciation
Stocking	чулок (m)	choo-**lok**
Stole	палантин(m)	pa-lan-**teen**
Suit	костюм (m)	kas-**tyoom**
Thread	нитка (f)	**neet**-ka
Tie	галстук (m)	**gahls**-took
Tie-clip	запонка (f)	**zah**-pan-ka
Tunic	туника (f)	too-**nee**-ka
Towel	полотенце (n)	pa-la-**tyen**-tse
Trousers	брюки (pl.), штаны (pl.)	**bryoo**-kee, shta-**ni**
Turban	тюрбан (m)	tyoor-**bahn**
Underpants	трусы (pl.)	troo-**si**
Veil	вуаль (f)	voo-**ahl'**
Worsted	шерстяная материя (f)	shir-stee-**nah**-ya ma-**tye**-ree-ya
Waistcoat	жилет (m)	zhi-**lyet**
Yarn	нить (f), пряжа (f)	neet', **pryah**-zha

Chapter-12

Numbers

Числа (cheesla)

	English	Russian	Pronunciation
1	one	один, раз	a-**deen**, rahs
2	two	два	dvah
3	three	три	tree
4	four	четыре	chee-**ti**-ree
5	five	пять	pyaht'
6	six	шесть	shest'
7	seven	семь	syem'
8	eight	восемь	**vo**-seem'
9	nine	девять	**dye**-veet'
10	ten	десять	**dye**-seet'
11	eleven	одиннадцать	a-**dee**-nat-tsat'
12	twelve	двенадцать	dvee-**naht**-tsat'
13	thirteen	тринадцать	tree-**naht**-tsat'
14	fourteen	четырнадцать	chee-**tir**-nat-tsat'
15	fifteen	пятнадцать	pyat-**naht**-tsat'
16	sixteen	шестнадцать	shis-**naht**-tsat'

	English	Russian	Pronunciation
17	seventeen	семнадцать	seem-**naht**-tsat'
18	eighteen	восемнадцать	va-seem-**naht**-tsat'
19	nineteen	девятнадцать	dee-veet-**naht**-tsat'
20	twenty	двадцать	**dvaht**-tsat'
21	twenty one	двадцать один	**dvaht**-tsat' a-**deen**
22	twenty two	двадцать два	**dvaht**-tsat' dvah
23	twenty three	двадцать три	**dvaht**-tsat' tree
24	twenty four	двадцать четыре	**dvaht**-tsat' chee-**ti**-ree
25	twenty five	двадцать пять	**dvaht**-tsat' pyaht'
26	twenty six	двадцать шесть	**dvaht**-tsat' shest'
27	twenty seven	двадцать семь	**dvaht**-tsat' syem'
28	twenty eight	двадцать восемь	**dvaht**-tsat' **vo**-seem'
29	twenty nine	двадцать девять	**dvaht**-tsat' **dye**-veet'
30	thirty	тридцать	**treet**-tstat'
31	thirty one	тридцать один	**treet**-tstat' a-**deen**
32	thirty two	тридцать два	**treet**-tstat' dvah
33	thirty three	тридцать три	**treet**-tstat' tree
34	thirty four	тридцать четыре	**treet**-tstat' chee-**ti**-ree
35	thirty five	тридцать пять	**treet**-tstat' pyaht'
36	thirty six\	тридцать шесть	**treet**-tstat' shest'
37	thirty seven	тридцать семь	**treet**-tstat' syem'

	English	Russian	Pronunciation
38	thirty eight	тридцать восемь	**treet**-tstat' **vo**-seem'
39	thirty nine	тридцать девять	**treet**-tstat' **dye**-veet'
40	forty	сорок	**so**-rak
41	forty one	сорок один	**so**-rak a-**deen**
42	forty two	сорок два	**so**-rak dvah
43	forty three	сорок три	**so**-rak tree
44	forty four	сорок четыре	**so**-rak chee-**ti**-ree
45	forty five	сорок пять	**so**-rak pyaht'
46	forty six	сорок шесть	**so**-rak shest'
47	forty seven	сорок семь	**so**-rak syem'
48	forty eight	сорок восемь	**so**-rak **vo**-seem'
49	forty nine	сорок девять	**so**-rak **dye**-veet'
50	fifty	пятьдесят	peed'-dee-**syaht**
51	fifty one	пятьдесят один	peed'-dee-**syaht** a-**deen**
52	fifty two	пятьдесят два	peed'-dee-**syaht** dvah
53	fifty three	пятьдесят три	peed'-dee-**syaht** tree
54	fifty four	пятьдесят четыре	peed'-dee-**syaht** chee-**ti**-ree
55	fifty five	пятьдесят пять	peed'-dee-**syaht** pyaht'
56	fifty six	пятьдесят шесть	peed'-dee-**syaht** shest'
57	fifty seven	пятьдесят семь	peed'-dee-**syaht** syem'
58	fifty eight	пятьдесят восемь	peed'-dee-**syaht** **vo**-seem'

	English	Russian	Pronunciation
59	fifty nine	пятьдесят девять	peed'-dee-**syaht** **dye**-veet'
60	sixty	шестьдесят	shiz-dee-**syaht**
61	sixty one	шестьдесят один	shiz-dee-**syaht** a-**deen**
62	sixty two	шестьдесят два	shiz-dee-**syaht** dvah
63	sixty three	шестьдесят три	shiz-dee-**syaht** tree
64	sixty four	шестьдесят четыре	shiz-dee-**syaht** chee-**ti**-ree
65	sixty five	шестьдесят пять	shiz-dee-**syaht** pyaht'
66	sixty six	шестьдесят шесть	shiz-dee-**syaht** shest'
67	sixty seven	шестьдесят семь	shiz-dee-**syaht** syem'
68	sixty eight	шестьдесят восемь	shiz-dee-**syaht** **vo**-seem'
69	sixty nine	шестьдесят девять	shiz-dee-**syaht** **dye**-veet'
70	seventy	семьдесят	**syem'**-dee-syat
71	seventy one	семьдесят один	**syem'**-dee-syat a-**deen**
72	seventy two	семьдесят два	**syem'**-dee-syat dvah
73	seventy three	семьдесят три	**syem'**-dee-syat tree
74	seventy four	семьдесят четыре	**syem'**-dee-syat chee-**ti**-ree
75	seventy five	семьдесят пять	**syem'**-dee-syat pyaht'

	English	Russian	Pronunciation
76	seventy six	семьдесят шесть	**syem'**-dee-syat shest'
77	seventy seven	семьдесят семь	**syem'**-dee-syat syem'
78	seventy eight	семьдесят восемь	**syem'**-dee-syat **vo**-seem'
79	seventy nine	семьдесят девять	**syem'**-dee-syat **dye**-veet'
80	eighty	восемьдесят	**vo**-seem-dee-syat
81	eighty one	восемьдесят один	**vo**-seem-dee-syat a-**deen**
82	eighty two	восемьдесят два	**vo**-seem-dee-syat dvah
83	eighty three	восемьдесят три	**vo**-seem-dee-syat tree
84	eighty four	восемьдесят четыре	**vo**-seem-dee-syat chee-**ti**-ree
85	eighty five	восемьдесят пять	**vo**-seem-dee-syat pyaht'
86	eighty six	восемьдесят шесть	**vo**-seem-dee-syat shest'
87	eighty seven	восемьдесят семь	**vo**-seem-dee-syat syem'
88	eighty eight	восемьдесят восемь	**vo**-seem-dee-syat **vo**-seem'
89	eighty nine	восемьдесят девять	**vo**-seem-dee-syat **dye**-veet'
90	ninety	девяносто	dee-vee-**nos**-ta
91	ninety one	девяносто один	dee-vee-**nos**-ta a-**deen**
92	ninety two	девяносто два	dee-vee-**nos**-ta dvah
93	ninety three	девяносто три	dee-vee-**nos**-ta tree

	English	Russian	Pronunciation
94	ninety four	девяносто четыре	dee-vee-**nos**-ta chee-**ti**-ree
95	ninety five	девяносто пять	dee-vee-**nos**-ta pyaht'
96	ninety six	девяносто шесть	dee-vee-**nos**-ta shest'
97	ninety seven	девяносто семь	dee-vee-**nos**-ta syem'
98	ninety eight	девяносто восемь	dee-vee-**nos**-ta **vo**-seem'
99	ninety nine	девяносто девять	dee-vee-**nos**-ta **dye**-veet'
100	hundred	сто	sto
101	hundred one	сто один	sto a-**deen**
200	two hundred	двести	**dvyes**-tee
1000	thousand	тысяча	**ti**-see-cha
1002	thousand and two	тысяча два	**ti**-see-cha dvah
2000	two thousand	две тысячи	dvye **ti**-see-chee
10000	ten thousand	десять тысяч	**dye**-syat' **ti**-seech
100000	hundred thousand	сто тысяч	sto **ti**-seech
1000000	million	миллион	mee-lee-**on**

Chapter-13

Money & Currency Exchange
Деньги и обмен валюты
(dyen'gee ee abmyen valyooti)

English	Russian	Pronunciation
Currency	валюта (f)	va-**lyoo**-ta
Currency market	валютный рынок (m)	va-**lyoot**-niy **ri**-nak
Currency note	купюра (f)	koo-**pyoo**-ra
Currency restrictions	валютные ограничения (pl.)	va-**lyoot**-ni-ye ag-ra-nee-**che**-nee-ya
Currency unit	валютная единица (f)	va-**lyoot**-na-ya yee-dee-**nee**-tsa
One dollar bill	купюра в один доллар (f)	koo-**pyoo**-ra v a-**deen dol**-lar
Dollar rate	курс доллара (m)	koors **dol**-la-ra
Dollar sign	знак доллара (m)	znahk **dol**-la-ra
Foreign exchange	обмен (иностранной) валюты (m)	ab-**myen** (ee-nas-**trahn**-nay) va-**lyoo**-ti
Exchange rate	валютный курс (m)	va-**lyoot**-niy chek
Traveller's cheque	туристский чек (m)	too-**reest**-skeey chek

Where can I change some money?
Где я могу поменять деньги?
Gdye yah ma-**goo** pa-mee-**nyaht' dyen'**-gee?

What is the exchange rate?
Какой валютный курс?
Ka-**koy** va-**lyoot**-niy koors?

I am out of cash. / I haven't any cash on me.
У меня нет наличных (денег).
Oo mee-**nyah** nyet na-**leech**-nih (**dye**-neek).

What's the charge for that?
Сколько это стоит?
Skol'-ka **e**-ta **sto**-eet?

You may keep the change.
Сдачи не надо.
Zdah-chee nye **nah**-da.

I would like to change money.
Я бы хотел(а) поменять деньги.
Yah bi kha-**tyel/tye**-la pa-mee-**nyaht' dyen'**-gee.

I would like to change a traveller's cheque.
Я бы хотел(а) поменять туристский чек.
Yah bi kha-**tyel/tye**-la pa-mee-**nyaht'** too-**reest**-skeey chek.

I would like to change 5.000 Rupees into Euros.
Я бы хотел(а) поменять 5.000 рупий на доллары.
Yah bi kha-**tyel/tye**-la pa-mee-**nyaht'** 5.000 **roo**-peey na **dol**-la-ri.

Where is the nearest ATM?
Где (находится) ближайший банкомат?
Gdye (na-**kho**-deet-sya) blee-**zhahy**-shiy ban-ka-**maht**?

Can I use my credit card to withdraw money?
Я могу снять деньги с кредитной карты?
Yah ma-**goo** snyaht' **dyen'**-gee s kree-**deet**-nay **kahr**-ti?

Can I have some coins/tokens?
Можно мне несколько монет/талонов?
Mozh-na mnye **nyes**-kal'-ka ma-**nyet**/ta-**lo**-naf?

Chapter-14

Time

Время (vryemya)

English	Russian	Pronunciation
Afternoon	после полудня	**pos**-lee pa-**lood**-nya
A quarter of...	четверть (f)	**chet**-veert'
An hour	час (m)	chahs
Anniversary	юбилей (m)	yoo-bee-**lyey**
At times	временами	vree-mee-**nah**-mee
A while	пока	pa-**kah**
Century	век (m)	vyek
Dawn	рассвет (m)	ras-**svyet**
Day	день (m)	dyen'
Day-to-day	повседневный	paf-seed-**nyev**-niy
Decade	десятилетие (n)	dee-see-tee-**lye**-tee-ye
Evening	вечер (m)	**vye**-cheer
Fortnight	две недели (pl.)	dvye nee-**dye**-lee
Golden jubilee	золотой	za-la-**toy**
	юбилей (m)	yoo-bee-**lyey**
Hour	час (m)	chahs

English	Russian	Pronunciation
Late	поздно	**poz**-na
Leap year	високосный год (m)	vee-sa-**kos**-niy got
Midday	полдень (m)	**pol**-deen'
Midnight	полночь (f)	**pol**-nach
Minute	минута (f)	mee-**noo**-ta
Morning	утро (n)	**oot**-ra
New year	новый год (m)	**no**-viy got
New years's eve	канун нового года (m)	ka-**noon** **no**-va-va **go**-da
Period	период (m)	pee-**ree**-at
Second	секунда (f)	see-**koon**-da
Silver jubilee	серебряный юбилей (m)	see-**ryeb**-ree-niy got
Sometimes	иногда	ee-nag-**dah**
Time	время (n)	**vrye**-mya

PRESENT Настоящее (nasta**yah**shcheeye)

Now	сейчас	see-**chahs**
Nowadays	теперь	tee-**pyer'**

English	Russian	Pronunciation
Right now	прямо сейчас	**pryah**-ma see-**chahs**
This afternoon	сегодня днем	see-**vod**-nya dnyom
This month	в этом месяце	v **e**-tam **mye**-see-tse
This morning	сегодня утром	see-**vod**-nya **oot**-ram
This week	на этой неделе	na **e**-tay nee-**dye**-lye
This year	в этом году	v **e**-tam ga-**doo**
Today	сегодня	see-**vod**-nya
Tonigt	сегодня вечером	see-**vod**-nya **vye**-chee-ram

PAST Прошлое (proshlaye)

Day before-yesterday	позавчера	pa-zaf-chee-**rah**
Last month	в прошлом месяце	f **prosh**-lam **mye**-see-tse
Last night	прошлой ночью	**prosh**-lay **noch'**-yoo
Last time	в прошлый раз	f **prosh**-liy rahs
Last week	на прошлой неделе	na **prosh**-lay nee-**dye**-lee
Last year	в прошлом году	f **prosh**-lahm ga-**doo**

English	Russian	Pronunciation
Since	с тех пор (как)	s tyekh por (kahk)
The year before	в позапрошлом году	f pa-za-**prosh**-lam ga-**doo**
Two days ago	два дня назад	dvah dnyah na-**zaht**
Yesterday	вчера	fchee-**rah**
Yesterday-afternoon	вчера днем	fchee-**rah** dnyom
Yesterday-evening	вчера вечером	fchee-**rah vye**-chee-ram
Yesterday-morning	вчера утром	fchee-**rah oot**-ram

FUTURE Будущее (boodooshcheeye)

Day after-tomorrow	послезавтра	**pos**-lee-**zahf**-tra
In a month	через месяц	**che**-rees **mye**-seets
In an hour	через час	**che**-rees chahs
In five minutes	через пять минут	**che**-rees pyaht' mee-**noot**
In two days	через два дня	**che**-rees dvah dnyah

English	Russian	Pronunciation
Next month	в следующем месяце	f **slye**-doo-shcheem **mye**-see-tse
Next week	на следующей неделе	na **slye**-doo-shcheey nee-**dye**-lee
Nest year	в следующем году	f **slye**-doo-shcheem ga-**doo**
Tomorrow	завтра	**zahft**-ra
Tomorrow-afternoon	завтра днем	**zahft**-ra dnyom
Tomorrow-evening	завтра вечером	**zahft**-ra **vye**-chee-ram
Tomorrow-morning	завтра утром	**zahft**-ra **oot**-ram
Until	до, пока не	do, pa-**kah** nye

What is the time?
Сколько времени?
Skol'-ka **vrye**-mee-nee?

It's 1 o'clock.
Час.
Chahs.

It's 2 o'clock.
Два часа.
Dvah cha-**sah**.

It's half past 9.
Половина десятого.
Pa-la-**vee**-na dee-**syah**-ta-va.

It's quarter past 8.
Четверть девятого.
Chet-veert' dee-**vyah**-ta-va.

It's quarter to six.
Без четверти шесть.
Byes **chet**-veer-tee shest'.

It's 10 to 7.
Без десяти 7 (семь).
Byes dee-see-**tee** 7 (syem').

At 10 a.m.
В 10 утра.
V 10 (**dye**-seet') oot-**rah**.

At 3 p.m. sharp.
Ровно в три (часа) дня.
Rov-na f tree (cha-**sah**) dnyah.

Note: a.m. is denoted by "утра" and p.m. by "дня" or "вечера".

3 (three) hours 20 (twenty) minutes and 10 (ten) seconds.
3 (три) часа 20 (двадцать) минут и 10 (десять) секунд.
3 (tree) cha-**sah** 20 (**dvaht**-tsat') mee-**noot** ee 10 (**dye**-seet') see-**koont**.

The train / bus leaves at 16.35.
Поезд / автобус отправляется в 16.35.
Po-yeest / af-**to**-boos at-prav-**lyah**-eet-sya f 16.35.

Until 10 (ten) o'clock.
До 10 (десяти) часов.
Do 10 (dee-see-**tee**) cha-**sof**.

'open / closed from... to...'
'открыто / закрыто с.. до...'
'at-**kri**-ta / zak-**ri**-ta s... do...'

It's late.
Поздно.
Poz-na.

Chapter-15

Week
Неделя (nee<u>dye</u>lya)

English	Russian	Pronunciation
Monday	понедельник (m)	pa-nee-**dyel'**-neek
Tuesday	вторник (m)	**ftor**-neek
Wednesday	среда (f)	sree-**dah**
Thursday	четверг (m)	cheet-**vyerk**
Friday	пятница (f)	**pyaht**-nee-tsa
Saturday	суббота (f)	soo-**bo**-ta
Sunday	воскресенье (n)	vas-kree-**syen'**-ye

Tomorrow is Friday.
Завтра пятница.
Zahf-tra **pyaht**-nee-tsa.

On Monday
В понедельник
F pa-nee-**dyel'**-neek

On Tuesdays
По вторникам.
Po **ftor**-nee-kam

Chapter-16

Months
Месяцы (myeseetsi)

English	Russian	Pronunciation
January	январь	yan-**vahr'**
February	февраль	feev-**rahl'**
March	март	mahrt
April	апрель	ap-**ryel'**
May	май	mahy
June	июнь	ee-**yoon'**
July	июль	ee-**yool'**
August	август	**ahv**-goost
September	сентябрь	seen-**tyahbr'**
October	октябрь	ak-**tyahbr'**
November	ноябрь	na-**yahbr'**
December	декабрь	dee-**kahbr'**

Chapter-17

Date

Число (cheeslo)

What is the date today?
Какое сегодня число?
Ka-**ko**-ye see-**vod**-nya chees-**lo**?

Today's the 23rd March.
Сегодня двадцать третье марта.
See-**vod**-nya **dvaht**-tsat **tryet'**-ye **mahr**-ta.

On the 3rd of this month/of next month.
Третьего числа этого месяца/следующего месяца.
Tryet'-yee-va chees-**lah e**-ta-va **mye**-see-tsa/**slye**-doo-shchee-va **mye**-see-tsa.

Until 6th May.
До шестого мая.
Do shees-**to**-va **mah**-ya.

Chapter-18

Hobbies
Хобби (khob-bee)

English	Russian	Pronunciation
Cooking	кулинарить	koo-lee-**nah**-reet'
Dancing	танцевать	tan-tsi-**vaht'**
Gardening	заниматься садоводством	za-nee-**maht**-sya sa-da-**vot**-stvam
Hiking	путешествовать	poo-tee-**shes**-tva-vat'
Pub crawls	посещать пабы	pa-see-**shchaht' pah**-bi
Reading	читать	chee-**taht'**
Shopping	делать шопинг	**dye**-lat' **sho**-peeng
Socializing	общаться	ap-**shchaht**-sya
Sport	заниматься спортом	za-nee-**maht**-sya **spor**-tam
Travelling	путешествовать	poo-tee-**shes**-tva-vat'

Do you like travelling?
Вы любите путешествовать?
Vi **lyoo-**bee-tye poo-tee-**shes**-tva-vat'?

Do you like playing an instrument?
Вы любите играть на музыкальных инструментах?
Vi **lyoo-**bee-tye eeg-**raht'** na moo-zi-**kahl'-**nih een-stroo-**myen-**takh?

Do you like singing?
Вы любите петь?
Vi **lyoo-**bee-tye pyet'?

Do you like listening to music?
Вы любите слушать музыку?
Vi **lyoo-**bee-tye **sloo-**shat' **moo-**zi-koo?

Do you like watching movies?
Вы любите смотреть кино?
Vi **lyoo-**bee-tye smat-**ryet'** kee-**no**?

Do you like going to concerts?
Вы любите ходить на концерты?
Vi **lyoo-**bee-tye kha-**deet'** na kan-**tser**-ti?

What music do you like?
Какую музыку вы любите?
Ka-**koo**-yoo **moo**-zi-koo vi **lyoo-**bee-tye?

Chapter-19

Relationships

Отношения (atnasheneeya)

English	Russian	Pronunciation
Adopted	приемный (m)/приемная (f)	pree-**yom**-niy (m)/pree-**yom**-na-ya (f)
Aunt	тетя	**tyo**-tya
Boyfriend	молодой человек, друг	ma-la-**doy** chee-la-**vyek**, drook
Bride	невеста	nee-**vyes**-ta
Bridegroom	жених	zhi-**neekh**
Brother	брат	braht
Brother-in-law	зять	zyaht'
Cousin	кузен (m)/кузина (f)	koo-**zen** (m)/koo-**zee**-na (f)
Daughter	дочь	doch
Daughter-in-law	невестка	nee-**vyest**-ka
Elder brother	старший брат	**stahr**-shiy braht
Elder sister	старшая сестра	**stahr**-sha-ya sees-**trah**

English	Russian	Pronunciation
Family	семья	seem'-**yah**
Father	папа	**pah**-pa
Father-in-law	свекор/тесть	**svyo**-kar/tyest'
Fiancé	жених	zhee-**neekh**
Fiancée	невеста	nee-**vyes**-ta
Girlfriend	девушка, подруга	**dye**-voosh-ka, pad-**roo**-ga
Grandchildren	внуки	**vnoo**-kee
Granddaughter	внучка	**vnooch**-ka
Grandparents	дедушка и бабушка	**dye**-doosh-ka ee **bah**-boosh-ka
Grandson	внук	vnook
Guest	гость	gost'
Host	хозяин	kha-**zyah**-een
Husband	муж	moosh
Mother	мама	**mah**-ma
Mother-in-law	свекровь / теща	sveek-**rof'**
Neighbour	сосед (m)	sa-**syet**
Nephew	племянник	plee-**myahn**-neek
Niece	племянница	plee-**myahn**-nee-tsa
Parents	родители	ra-**dee**-tee-lee

English	Russian	Pronunciation
Relative	родственник (m)	**rot**-stveen-neek
Sister	сестра	sees-**trah**
Son	сын	sin
Son-in-law	зять	zyaht'
Spouse	супруг (m)	soop-**rook** (m) /
	/ супруга (f)	soop-**roo**-ga (f)
Twin brother/sister	близнец	bleez-**nyets**
Uncle	дядя	**dyah**-dya
Wedding	свадьба (f)	**svahd'**-ba
Widow	вдова	vda-**vah**
Widower	вдовец	vda-**vyets**
Wife	жена	zhi-**nah**
Younger brother	младший брат	**mlaht**-sheey braht
Yonger sister	младшая сестра	**mlaht**-sha-ya sees-**trah**

Chapter-20

Sport

Спорт (sport)

English	Russian	Pronunciation
Abseiling	альпинизм (m)	al'-pee-**neezm**
Ace	очко (n)	ach-**ko**
Athlete	атлет (m)	at-**lyet**
Badminton	бадминтон (m)	bad-meen-**ton**
Ball	мяч (m)	myahch
Basketball	баскетбол (m)	bas-keet-**bol**
Bat	бита (f)	**bee**-ta
Bungee-jumping	прыжок с тросом (m)	pri-**zhok** s **tro**-sam
Bullfight	бой быков (m)	boy bi-**kof**
Card-game	карточная игра (f)	**kahr**-tach-na-ya eeg-**rah**
Caving	изучение пещер (n)	ee-zoo-**che**-nee-ye pee-**shcher**
Champion	чемпион (m)	cheem-pee-**on**
Championship	чемпионат (m)	cheem-pee-a-**naht**

English	Russian	Pronunciation
Coach	тренер (m)	**trye**-neer
Corner	угловой удар (m)	oog-la-**voy** oo-**dahr**
Cricket	крикет (m)	kree-**kyet**
Cricketer	игрок в крикет (m)	eeg-**rok** f kree-**kyet**
Cycling	велоспорт (m)	**vye**-la-**sport**
Defeat	поражение (f)	pa-ra-**zhe**-nee-ye
Free kick	свободный удар (m)	sva-**bod**-niy oo-**dahr**
Football	футбол (m)	foot-**bol**
Foul	фол (m)	fol
Game	игра (f)	eeg-**rah**
Game fishing	рыбалка (f)	ri-**bahl**-ka
Goal	гол (m)	gol
Goal keeper	голкипер (m)	gal-**kee**-peer
Golf	гольф (m)	gol'f
Group	группа (f)	**groop**-pa
Hockey	хоккей (f)	kha-**kyey**
Judo	дзюдо (n)	dzyoo-**do**
Karate	каратэ (n)	ka-ra-**te**
Ludo	лудо (n)	loo-**do**
Match	матч (m)	mahtch

English	Russian	Pronunciation
Mountain-	горный	**gor**-niy
biking	велосипед (m)	vee-la-see-**pyet**
Offside	вне игры	vnye eeg-**ri**
Penalty	пенальти (n)	pee-**nahl'**-tee
Pass	пас (m)	pahs
Player	игрок (m)	eeg-**rok**
Playground	площадка (f)	pla-**shchaht**-ka
Racket	ракетка (f)	ra-**kyet**-ka
Rock climbing	скалолазание (n)	ska-la-**lah**-za-nee-ye
Serve	подача (f)	pa-**dah**-cha
Snakes-	змейки	**zmyey**-kee
ladders	и лесенки (pl.)	ee **lye**-seen-kee
Sportsman	спортсмен (m)	spart-**smyen**
Surfing	серфинг (m)	**syor**-feeng
Swimmer	пловец (m)	pla-**vyets**
Swimming	плавание (n)	**plah**-va-nee-ye
Team	команда (f)	ka-**mahn**-da
Tennis	теннис (m)	**te**-nees
Tennis-court	теннисный корт (m)	**te**-nees-niy kort
Victory	победа (f)	pa-**bye**-da

English	Russian	Pronunciation
Volleyball	волейбол (m)	va-leey-**bol**
Water-skis	водные лыжи (pl.)	**vod**-ni-ye **li**-zhi
Winner	победитель (m)	pa-bee-**dee**-teel'
Wrestling	борьба (f)	bar'-**bah**

Do you like sport?
Ты любишь спорт?
Ti **lyoo**-beesh sport?

Yes, very much.
Да, очень.
Da, **o**-cheen'.

Not really.
Нет.
Nyet.

Would you like to go to a cricket match?
Ты бы хотел(а) пойти на крикет?
Ti bi kha-**tyel**/kha-**tye**-la pay-**tee** na kree-**kyet**?

What is the score now?
Какой сейчас счет?
Ka-**koy** see-**chahs** shchot?

It's a draw/love.
Ничья.
Neech-**yah**.

It's a match-point.
Матч-поинт.
Mahtch - **po**-eent.

How much time is left?
Сколько осталось времени?
Skol'-ka as-**tah**-las' **vrye**-mee-nee?

What sport do you play?
Каким спортом ты занимаешься?
Ka-**keem spor**-tam ti za-nee-**mah**-yeesh-sya?

I play...
Я занимаюсь...
Yah za-nee-**mah**-yoos'...

Who's your favourite sportsman?
Кто твой любимый спортсмен?
Kto tvoy lyoo-**bee**-miy sparts-**myen**?

I follow...
Я болею за...
Yah ba-**lye**-yoo za...

I like watching sport.
Я люблю смотреть спорт.
Yah lyoob-**lyoo** smat-**ryet'** sport.

Who plays for Real Madrid?
Кто играет за Реал Мадрид?
Kto eeg-**rah**-eet za Ree-**ahl** Mad-**reet**?

Which team is at the top of the league?
Какая команда лидирует в лиге?
Ka-**kah**-ya ka-**mahn**-da lee-**dee**-roo-eet v **lee**-gee?

Which team are you supporting?
За какую команду ты болеешь?
Za ka-**koo**-yoo ka-**mahn**-doo ti ba-**lye**-eesh?

That was a great match!
Отличный матч!
At-**leech**-niy mahtch!

Do you want to play?
Ты хочешь поиграть?
Ti **kho**-cheesh pa-eeg-**raht'**?

Can I join in?
Можно с вами?
Mozh-na s **vah**-mee?

Can I hire a racquet?
Можно взять на прокат ракетку?
Mozh-na vzyaht' na pra-**kaht** ra-**kyet**-koo?

What's the charge per day?
Какой тариф за день?
Ka-**koy** ta-**reef** za dyen'?

What's the charge per hour?
Какой тариф за час?
Ka-**koy** ta-**reef** za chahs?

I would like to scuba diving?
Я бы хотел(а) пойти на скуба-дайвинг.
Yah bi kha-**tyel**/kha-**tye**-la pay-**tee** na **skoo**-ba **dahy**-veenk.

I would like to learn to dive.
Я бы хотел(а) научиться дайвингу.
Yah bi kha-**tyel**/kha-**tye**-la na-oo-**cheet**-sya **dahy**-veen-goo.

Where are some good diving sites?
Где хорошие места для дайвинга?
Gdye kha-**ro**-shee-ye mees-**tah** dlya **dahy**-veen-ga?

Are you sure this is safe?
Вы уверены, что это безопасно?
Vi oo-**vye**-ree-ni shto **e**-ta bee-za-**pahs**-na?

Chapter-21

Ailments
Болезни (balyeznee)

English	Russian	Pronunciation
Accident	авария (f)	a-**vah**-ree-ya
Acidity	кислотность (f)	kees-**lot**-nast'
Acne	прыщи (pl.)	pri-**shchi**
AIDS	СПИД (m)	speed
AIDS test	тест на СПИД (m)	test na speed
Ailments	заболевания (pl.)	za-ba-lee-**vah**-nee-ya
Allergy	аллергия (f)	a-leer-**gee**-ya
Ambulance	скорая помощь (f)	**sko**-ra-ya **po**-mashch
Anesthetic	анестезия (f)	a-nes-te-**zee**-ya
Antibiotics	антибиотики (pl.)	an-tee-bee-**o**-tee-kee
Antihistamines	антифитамины (pl.)	an-tee-fee-ta-**mee**-ni
Anti inflammatory	противовосп алительный	**pro**-tee-va-vas-pa-**lee**-teel'-niy

English	Russian	Pronunciation
Appendicitis	аппендицит (m)	ap-peen-dee-**cit**
Aspirin	аспирин (m)	as-pee-**reen**
Asthma	астма (f)	**ahs**-ma
Baldness	облысение (n)	ab-li-**sye**-nee-ye
Bandage	бинт (m)	beent
Belching	отрыжка (f)	at-**rish**-ka
Bile	желчь (f)	zhelch
Bleeding	кровотечение (n)	kra-va-tee-**che**-nee-ye
Blindness	слепота (f)	slee-pa-**tah**
Blister	волдырь (m)	val-**dir'**
Blood	кровь (f)	krof'
Blood flow	кровотечение (n)	**kro**-va-tee-**che**-nee-ye
Blood group	группа крови (f)	**groop**-pa **kro**-vee
Blood-poisoning	сепсис (m), заражение крови (n)	**syep**-sees, za-ra-**zhe**-nee-ye **kro**-vee
Blood pressure	кровяное давление (n)	kra-vee-**no**-ye dav-**lye**-nee-ye
Breath	дыхание (n)	di-**khah**-nee-ye

English	Russian	Pronunciation
Bronchitis	бронхит (m)	bran-**kheet**
Bruise	синяк (m)	see-**nyahk**
Burn	ожог (m)	a-**zhok**
Cardiac	остановка	as-ta-**nof**-ka
arrest	сердца (f)	**syer**-tsa
Casualty	отделение	ad-dee-**lye**-nee-ye
department	скорой помощи (n)	**sko**-ray **po**-ma-shchee
Cataract	катаракта (f)	ka-ta-**rahk**-ta
Chemotherapy	химиотерапия (f)	**khee**-mee-a-te-ra-**pee**-ya
Chickenpox	ветряная оспа (f)	veet-ree-**nah**-ya **os**-pa
Chilblain	опухание (n)	a-poo-**khah**-nee-ye
Chill	обморожение (n)	ab-ma-ra-**zhe**-nee-ye
Cholera	холера (f)	kha-**lye**-ra
Clinic	клиника (f)	**klee**-nee-ka
Colic	колик (m)	**ko**-leek
Concussion	сотрясение (n)	sat-rya-**sye**-nee-ye
Condom	презерватив (m)	pree-zeer-va-**teef**
Conjunctivitis	конъюнктивит (m)	kan'-yook-tee-**veet**

English	Russian	Pronunciation
Constipation	запор (m)	za-**por**
Consumption	туберкулез (m)	too-beer-koo-**lyos**
Contact	контактные	kan-**tahkt**-ni-ye
lenses	линзы (pl.)	**leen**-zi
Contagious	заразный	za-**rahz**-niy
Cough	кашель (m)	**kah**-shil'
Cramp	спазм (m)	spazm
Cure	лечение (n)	lee-**che**-nee-ye
Cystitis	цистит (m)	tsis-**teet**
Depressed	подавленный	pa-**dahv**-leen-niy
Dermatologist	дерматолог (m)	der-ma-**to**-lag
Diabetes	диабет (m)	dee-a-**byet**
Diagnosis	диагноз (m)	dee-**ahg**-nas
Diarrhea	диарея (f)	dee-a-**rye**-ya
Disease	болезнь (f)	ba-**lyezn'**
Dispensary	диспансер (m)	dees-pan-**ser**
Doctor	доктор (m),	**dok**-tar, vrahch
	врач (m)	
Dose	доза (f)	**do**-za

English	Russian	Pronunciation
Drugstore	аптека (f)	ap-**tye**-ka
Dumbness	немота (f)	nee-ma-**tah**
Dwarf	карлик (m)	**kahr**-leek
Dysentery	дизентерия (f)	dee-zeen-tee-**ree**-ya
Eczema	экзема (f)	eeg-**ze**-ma
ENT	ухо-горло-нос	**oo**-kha **gor**-la - nos
Epidemic	эпидемия (f)	ee-pee-**dye**-mee-ya
Epilepsy	эпилепсия (f)	ee-pee-**lyep**-see-ya
Faint	обморок (m)	**ob**-ma-rak
Fever	жар (m)	zhahr
Filling	сытный	**sit**-niy
First aid	первая	**pyer**-vah-ya
	помощь (f)	**po**-mashch
Flu	грипп (m)	greep
Food-	пищевое	pee-shchee-**vo**-ye
poisoning	отравление (n)	at-rav-**lye**-nee-ye
Fungal	грибковый	greep-**ko**-viy

English	Russian	Pronunciation
Gall-bladder	желчный пузырь (m)	**zhelch**-niy poo-**zir'**
Giddiness	головокружение (n)	ga-la-va-kroo-**zhe**-nee-ye
Gland	гланды (pl.)	**glahn**-di
Glasses	очки (pl.)	ach-**kee**
Gonorrhea	гонорея (f)	ga-na-**rye**-ya
Grip	спазм (m), судорога (f)	spahzm, **soo**-da-ra-ga
Gynecologist	гинеколог (m)	gee-nee-**ko**-lak
Have cold	простудиться	pras-too-**deet**-sya
Headache	головная боль (f)	ga-lav-**nah**-ya bol'
Heart	сердце (n)	**syer**-tse
Heart-attack	сердечный приступ (m)	seer-**dyech**-niy **prees**-toop
Hernia	грыжа (f)	**gri**-zha
Hiccup	икота (f)	ee-**ko**-ta
High blood-pressure	высокое кровяное давление (n)	vi-**so**-ka-ye kra-vee-**nos**-na-ye

English	Russian	Pronunciation
HIV negative	ВИЧ нет	veech nyet
HIV positive	ВИЧ есть	veech yest'
Homeopathy	гомеопатия (f)	ga-mee-a-**pah**-tee-ya
Hospital	госпиталь (m), больница (f)	**gos**-pee-tal', bal'-**nee**-tsa
Hunger	голод (m)	**go**-lat
Indigestion	несварение (желудка) (n)	nees-va-**rye**-nee-ye (zhi-**loot**-ka)
Infection	инфекция (f)	een-**fyek**-tsi-ya
Inflammation	воспаление (n)	vas-pa-**lye**-nee-ye
Inhaler	ингалятор (m)	een-ga-**lyah**-tar
Injection	инъекция (f)	een'-**yek**-tsi-ya
Injury	рана (f)	**rah**-na
Insomnia	бессонница (f)	bees-**son**-nee-tsa
Jaundice	желтуха (f)	zhil-**too**-kha
Kidney stone	камни в почках (pl.)	**kahm**-nee f **poch**-kakh
Leprosy	проказа (f)	pra-**kah**-za
Leukemia	лейкемия (f)	leey-kee-**mee**-ya

English	Russian	Pronunciation
Madness	сумасшествие (n)	soo-ma-**shest**-vee-ye
Measles	корь (f)	kor'
Medicine	лекарство (n)	lee-**kahrs**-tva
Menstruation	менструация (f)	meen-stroo-**ah**-tsi-ya
Migraine	мигрень (f)	meeg-**ryen'**
Mumps	свинка (f)	**sveen**-ka
Nausea	тошнота (f)	tash-na-**tah**
Nosebleed	кровь из носа (f)	krof' eez **no**-sa
Operate	оперировать	a-pee-**ree**-ra-vat'
Pain	боль (f)	bol'
Pediatrician	педиатр (m)	pee-dee-**ahtr**
Paralysis	паралич (m)	pa-ra-**leech**
Penicillin	пенициллин (m)	pee-nee-tsi-**leen**
Pharmacy	аптека (f)	ap-**tye**-ka
Piles	геморрой (m)	gee-ma-**roy**
Plaster	пластырь (m)	**plahs**-tir'
Plug	пробка (f)	**prop**-ka
Pneumonia	пневмония (f)	pneev-ma-**nee**-ya

English	Russian	Pronunciation
Pregnant	беременная	bee-**rye**-meen-na-ya
Prescription	рецепт (m)	ree-**tsept**
Pull muscle	растянуть	ras-tya-**noot'**
	мышцу	**mish**-tsoo
Pulse	пульс (m)	pool's
Pus	гной (m)	gnoy
Rheumatism	ревматизм (m)	reev-ma-**teezm**
Roundworm	круглый глист (m)	**kroog**-liy gleest
Saliva	слюна (f)	slyoo-**nah**
Sanitary-	санитарная	sa-nee-**tahr**-na-ya
napkin	салфетка (f)	sal-**fyet**-ka
Shiver	дрожь (f)	drosh
Shivery	дрожащий	dra-**zhah**-shchiy
Shock	шок (m)	shok
Short sight	близорукость (f)	blee-za-**roo**-kast'
Sick	больной	bal'-**noy**
Side effect	побочный	pa-**boch**-niy
	эффект (m)	ee-**fyekt**
Sinusitis	синусит (m)	see-noo-**seet**

English	Russian	Pronunciation
Sleeping pill	снотворное (n)	snat-**vor**-na-ye
Sneeze	чихание (n)	chi-**khah**-nee-ye
Sore throat	ангина (f)	an-**gee**-na
Sprain	растяжение	ras-tee-**zhe**-nee-ye
	связок (n)	**svyah**-zak
Sting	острая боль (f)	**os**-tra-ya bol'
Stomachache	боль в животе (f)	bol' v zhi-va-**tye**
Stool	стул (m)	stool
Sunburn	солнечный	**sol**-neech-niy
	ожог (m)	a-**zhok**
Sunstroke	солнечный	**sol**-neech-niy
	удар (m)	oo-**dahr**
Surgery	хирургия (f),	khee-roor-**gee**-ya,
	операция (f)	a-pee-**rah**-tsi-ya
Sweat	пот (m)	pot
Swelling	опухоль (f)	**o**-poo-khal'
Syringe	шприц (m)	shpreets
Tablet	таблетка (f)	tab-**lyet**-ka
Tetanus	столбняк (m)	stalb-**nyahk**

English	Russian	Pronunciation
Thermometer	термометр (m)	teer-**mo**-meetr
Treatment	лечение (n)	lee-**che**-nee-ye
Tumor	опухоль (m)	o-poo-**khat'**
Typhus	тиф (m)	teef
Urine	моча (f)	ma-**chah**
Vaccination	прививка оспы (f),	pree-**veef**-ka **os**-pi,
	вакцинация (f)	vak-tsi-**nah**-tsi-ya
Visiting hours	часы приема (pl.)	cha-**si** pree-**yo**-ma
Vomiting	рвота (f)	**rvo**-ta
Ward	палата (f)	pa-**lah**-ta
Weak	слабый	**slah**-biy
Wheelchair	инвалидное	een-va-**leed**-na-ye
	кресло (n)	**kryes**-la
Wound	рана (f)	**rah**-na
X-ray	рентген (m)	reen-**gyen**

Where is the pharmacy/clinic?
Где находится аптека/больница?
Gdye na-**kho**-deet-sya ap-**tye**-ka/bal'-**nee**-tsa?

English	Russian	Pronunciation

Is there a night chemist nearby?

Здесь есть круглосуточная аптека поблизости?

Zdyes' yest' kroog-la-**soo**-tach-na-ya ap-**tye**-ka pab-**lee**-zas-tee?

Is there a chemist nearby?

Здесь есть аптека поблизости?

Zdyes' yest' ap-**tye**-ka pab-**lee**-zas-tee?

Where is the nearest hospital?

Где ближайшая больница?

Gdye blee-**zhahy**-sha-ya bal'-**nee**-tsa?

Where is the Casualty?

Где отделение скорой помощи?

Gdye ad-dee-**lye**-nee-ye **sko**-ray **po**-ma-shchi?

What are the visiting hours?

Какие часы приема?

Ka-**kee**-ye cha-**si** pree-**yo**-ma?

English	Russian	Pronunciation

Where is ward no 6?

Где палата номер шесть?

Gdye pa-**lah**-ta **no**-meer shest'?

I need the medicine, please.

Дайте мне лекарство, пожалуйста.

Dahy-tye mnye lee-**kahr**-stva, pa-**zhah**-loos-ta.

Please give me medicine to cure..

Дайте, пожалуйста, мне лекарство от/для..

Dahy-tye, pa-**zhah**-loos-ta, mnye lee-**kahr**-stva ot/dlya..

Is it available only on prescription?

Это выдается только по рецепту?

E-ta vi-da-**yot**-sya **tol'**-ka pa ree-**tsep**-too?

I have the prescription.

У меня есть рецепт.

Oo mee-**nyah** yest' ree-**tsept**.

How many times a day?

Сколько раз в день?

Skol'-ka rahs v dyen'?

Twice a day

Два раза в день

Dvah **rah**-za v dyen'

Have you taken this before?

Ты принимал это раньше?

Ti pree-nee-**mahl e**-ta **rahn'**-she?

It is made according to prescription.

Это сделано по рецепту.

E-ta **zdye**-la-na po ree-**tsep**-too.

Can you order this medicine for me?

Ты можешь заказать это лекарство для меня?

Ti **mo**-zhish za-ka-**zaht' e**-ta lee-**kahr**-stva dlya mee-**nyah**?

When can I pick it up?

Когда я могу его забрать?

Kag-**dah** yah ma-**goo** ee-**vo** zab-**raht'**?

It will be ready to pick up in 15 minutes.

Его можно будет забрать через пятнадцать минут.

Ee-**vo mozh**-na **boo**-deet zab-**raht' che**-rees pyat-**naht**-tsat' mee-**noot**.

I feel sick.

Я болею.

Yah ba-**lye**-yoo.

I suffer from boils.

У меня фурункулы.

Oo mee-**nyah** foo-**roon**-koo-li.

I feel ill.

Я болею.

Yah ba-**lye**-yoo.

I suffer from rheumatism.

У меня ревматизм.

Oo mee-**nyah** reev-ma-**teezm**.

You can buy it over the counter.

Вы можете оплатить в кассе.

Vi **mo**-zhi-tye ap-la-**teet'** f **kahs**-sye.

Please get the doctor.

Пожалуйста, позовите врача.

Pa-**zhah**-loos-ta, pa-za-**vee**-tye vra-**chah**.

Quickly! Help! Medical care!

Скорее! На помощь! Врачи!

Ska-**rye**-ye! Na **po**-mashch! Vra-**chee**!

Can I see a female doctor?

Я могу попасть к доктору-женщине?

Yah ma-**goo** pa-**pahst'** k **dok**-ta-roo - **zhen**-shchi-nye?

I can't help coughing.

Мой кашель не проходит.

Moy **kah**-shil' nye pra-**kho**-deet.

Are you on medication?

Ты лечишься?

Ti **lye**-chish-sya?

I am on regular medication for...

Я лечусь от...

Yah lee-**choos'** ot...

It would be helpful if you could come and see the patient.

Вы очень поможете, если придете посмотреть пациента.

Vi **o**-cheen' pa-**mo**-zhi-tye, **yes**-lee pree-**dyo**-tye pas-mat-**ryet'** pa-tsi-**en**-ta.

Which doctor is treating you?

Какой врач тебя лечит?

Ka-**koy** vrahch tee-**byah lye**-cheet?

I can not tolerate the heat.

Я не выношу жару.

Yah nye vi-na-**shoo** zha-**roo**.

The doctor prescribed complete rest.

Доктор прописал полный покой.

Dok-tar pra-pee-**sahl pol**-niy pa-**koy**.

I will prescribe you a preventive medicine.

Я пропишу вам профилактическое лекарство.

Ya pra-pee-**shoo** vahm pra-fee-lak-**tee**-chis-ka-ye lee-**kahr**-stva.

He hurt his hand.

Он поранил/ушиб руку.

On pa-**rah**-neel/oo-**ship roo**-koo.

I have a toothache.

У меня болит зуб.

Oo mee-**nyah** ba-**leet** zoop.

Where does it hurt you?

Где у тебя ушиб?

Gdye oo tee-**byah** oo-**ship**?

My head aches.

У меня болит голова.

Oo mee-**nyah** ba-**leet** ga-la-**vah**.

I don't have an appetite.

У меня нет аппетита.

Oo mee-**nyah** nyet ap-pee-**tee**-ta.

My stomach aches.

У меня болит живот.

Oo mee-**nyah** ba-**leet** zhi-**vot**.

Does it hurt much?

Ты сильно ударился/ударилась?

Ti **seel'**-na oo-**dah**-reel-sya/oo-**dah**-ree-las'?

How do you feel?

Как ты себя чувствуешь?

Kak ti see-**byah** **choos**-tvoo-yesh?

I am constipated.

У меня запор.

Oo mee-**nyah** za-**por**.

I am dehydrated.

У меня обезвоживание.

Oo mee-**nyah** a-beez-**vo**-zhi-va-nee-ye.

I fell down the stairs.

Я упал(а) с лестницы.

Yah oo-**pahl**/oo-**pah**-la s **lyes**-nee-tsi?

That made me sick.

Поэтому мне плохо.

Pa-**e**-ta-moo mnye **plo**-kha.

Do you take drugs?

Ты принимаешь лекарства?

Ti pree-nee-**mah**-yeesh lee-**kahrs**-tva?

Can I see someone who practices naturopathy?

Мне нужен кто-нибудь, кто занимается натуропатией.

Mnye **noo**-zhin **kto**-nee-**boot'**, kto za-nee-**mah**-yeet-sya na-**too**-ra-**pah**-tee-yey.

I am on the pill.

Я на таблетках.

Yah na tab-**lyet**-kah.

I have been injured.

Я поранился/поранилась.

Yah pa-**rah**-neel-sya/pa-**rah**-nee-las'.

I have a case history of...

У меня история болезни...

Oo mee-**nyah** ees-**to**-ree-ya ba-**lyez**-nee...

You need to be admitted to hospital.

Тебе нужно в больницу.

Tee-**bye noozh**-na v bal'-**nee**-tsoo.

He needs a blood transfusion.

Ему нужно переливание крови.

Yee-**moo noozh**-na pee-ree-lee-**vah**-nee-ye **kro**-vee.

What is your blood group?

Какая у тебя группа крови?

Ka-**kah**-ya oo tee-**byah groop**-pa **kro**-vee?

Can you donate blood?

Ты можешь стать донором крови?

Ti **mo**-zhish staht' **do**-na-ram **kro**-vee?

Please use a new syringe.

Пожалуйста, используйте новый шприц.

Pa-**zhah**-loos-ta, ees-**pol'**-zooy-tye **no**-viy shpreets.

I think I am pregnant.

Кажется, я беременна.

Kah-zhit-sya, yah bee-**rye**-meen-na.

Are you using contraception?

Вы используете контрацептивы?

Vi ees-**pol'**-zoo-yee-tye kan-tra-tsip-**tee**-vi?

Chapter-22

Around the Town
В городе (v goradye)

English	Russian	Pronunciation
Airport	аэропорт (m)	a-ee-ra-**port**
Amusement-park	парк аттракционов (m)	pahrk at-trak-tsi-**o**-naf
Antique shop	антикварный магазин (m)	an-tee-**kvahr**-niy ma-ga-**zeen**
A one day excursion	однодневная экскурсия (f)	ad-na-**dnyev**-na-ya eeks-**koor**-see-ya
Area	зона (f)	**zo**-na
Bakery	булочная (f)	**boo**-lach-na-ya
Bar	бар (m)	bahr
Barber shop	парикмахерская (f)	pa-reekh-**mah**-kheer-ska-ya
Bazaar	рынок, базар (m)	**ri**-nak, ba-**zahr**

English	Russian	Pronunciation
Beach	пляж (m)	plyahzh
Beauty parlour	салон красоты (m)	sa-**lon** kra-sa-**ti**
Bicycle	велосипед (m)	vee-la-see-**pyet**
Boarding house	пансион (m)	pan-see-**on**
Boating trip	круиз (m)	kroo-**eez**
Bookshop	книжный	**kneezh**-niy
	магазин (m)	ma-ga-**zeen**
Border	граница (m)	gra-**nee**-tsa
Botanical garden	ботанический сад (m)	ba-ta-**nee**-chis-keey saht
Bridge	мост (m)	most
Building	здание (n)	**zdah**-nee-ye
Bus	автобус (m)	af-**to**-boos
Butcher's	мясной	myas-**noy**
shop	магазин (m)	ma-ga-**zeen**
Café	кафе (n)	ka-**fe**
Camping-	палаточный	**lah**-geer'
ground	лагерь (m)	pa-**lah**-tach-niy
Candy store	кондитерская (f)	kan-**dee**-teer-ska-ya

English	Russian	Pronunciation
Capital city	столица (f)	sta-**lee**-tsa
Carpenter	плотник (m)	**plot**-neek
Cart	телега (f)	tee-**lye**-ga
Casino	казино (n)	ka-zee-**no**
Castle	замок (m)	**zah**-mok
Cathedral	собор (m)	sa-**bor**
Cave	пещера (f)	pee-**shche**-ra
Chemist shop	аптека (f)	ap-**tye**-ka
Chinatown	чайнатаун (m)	**chahy**-na-**tah**-oon
Church	церковь (f)	**tser**-kaf′
Club	клуб (m)	kloop
Cinema	кино (n)	kee-**no**
Circus	цирк (m)	tsirk
City	город (m)	**go**-rat
City center	центр города (m)	tsentr **go**-ra-da
Coffee shop	кафе (n)	ka-**fe**
Concert	концерт (m)	kan-**tsert**
Consulate	консульство (n)	**kon**-sool′-stva

English	Russian	Pronunciation
Corner shop	угловой магазин (m)	oog-la-**voy** ma-ga-**zeen**
Cornet	корнет (m)	kar-**net**
Country club	загородный клуб (m)	**zah**-ga-rad-niy kloop
Country cottage	загородный коттедж (m)	**zah**-ga-rad-niy ka-**tetsh**
Country road	загородная дорога (f)	**zah**-ga-rad-na-ya da-**ro**-ga
Countryside	загородная местность (f)	**zah**-ga-rad-na-ya **myes**-nast'
Court (law)	суд (m)	soot
Crowd	толпа (f)	tal-**pah**
Dairy farm	молочная ферма (f)	ma-**loch**-na-ya **fyer**-ma
Dead end	тупик (m)	too-**peek**
Department store	универмаг (m)	oo-nee-veer-**mahg**
Discotheque	дискотека (f)	dees-ka-**tye**-ka
District	район (m)	ra-**yon**

English	Russian	Pronunciation
Ditch (road)	канава (f)	ka-**nah**-va
Drugstore	аптека (f)	ap-**tye**-ka
Dry-cleaner's	химчистка (f)	kheem-**chist**-ka
Electrician	электрик (m)	ee-**lyek**-treek
Embassy	посольство (n)	pa-**sol'**-stva
Excursion	экскурсия (f)	eeks-**koor**-see-ya
Excursion-train	экскурсионный поезд (m)	eeks-**koor**-see-on-niy **po**-yeest
Exhibition	выставка (f)	**vis**-taf-ka
Factory	фабрика (f), завод (m)	**fahb**-ree-ka
Farm	ферма (f)	**fyer**-ma
Farmhouse	дом на ферме (m)	dom na **fyer**-mye
Fence	ограда (f)	ag-**rah**-da
Field	поле (n)	**po**-lye
Fire-department	пожарный отдел (m)	pa-**zhahr**-niy ad-**dyel**
Fishing	рыбалка (f)	ri-**bahl**-ka
Fish market	рыбный рынок (m)	**rib**-niy **ri**-nak

English	Russian	Pronunciation
Flea market	открытый рынок (m)	at-**kri**-tiy **ri**-nak
Flower shop	цветочный	tsvee-**toch**-niy
	магазин (m)	ma-ga-**zeen**
Flower-show	выставка цветов (f)	**vis**-taf-ka tsvee-**tof**
Fort	форт (m)	fort
Fortress	крепость (f)	**krye**-past'
Fountain	фонтан (m)	fan-**tahn**
Fruit shop	фруктовый	frook-**to**-viy
	магазин (m)	ma-ga-**zeen**
Furniture	мебельный	**mye**-beel'-niy
shop	магазин (m)	ma-ga-**zeen**
Gallery (art)	галерея	ga-lee-**rye**-ya
	(искусства) (f)	(ees-**koos**-tva)
Garden	сад (m)	saht
Gate	ворота (pl.)	va-**ro**-ta
Golf-course	поле для гольфа (n)	**po**-lye dlya **gol'**-fa
Granary	зерносклад (m)	**zyer**-na-**sklaht**
Grave	могила (f)	ma-**gee**-la

English	Russian	Pronunciation
Greengrocer's-	овощная/	a-vashch-**nah**-ya/
shop	фруктовая	frook-**to**-va-ya
	лавка (f)	**lahf**-ka
Grocer's shop	бакалейный	ba-ka-**lyey**-niy
	магазин (m)	ma-ga-**zeen**
Guesthouse	гестхаус (m),	gyest-**khah**-oos,
	отель (m)	a-**tel'**
Gutter	сточная канава (f)	**stoch**-na-ya ka-**nah**-va
Harbour	гавань (f)	**gah**-van'
Hardware	хозяйственный	kha-**zyahy**-stveen-niy
shop	магазин (m)	ma-ga-**zeen**
Hat shop	шляпный	**shlyahp**-niy
	магазин (m)	ma-ga-**zeen**
High-rise	высотное	vi-**sot**-na-ye
building	здание (n),	**zda**-nee-ye (n),
	высотка (f)	vi-**sot**-ka (f)
Highway	шоссе (n),	shas-**se,**
	хайвей (m)	khay-**vey**
Hill	холм (m)	kholm

English	Russian	Pronunciation
Hospital	больница (f),	bal'-**nee**-tsa,
	госпиталь (m)	**gos**-pee-tal'
Hotel	отель (m),	a-**tel'**,
	гостиница (f)	gas-**tee**-nee-tsa
House	дом (m)	dom
Hut	хата (f)	**khah**-ta
Inn	дом (m),	dom, gas-**tee**-nee-tsa
	гостиница (f)	
Jewellery	магазин	ma-ga-**zeen**
shop	драгоценностей (m)	dra-ga-**tsen**-nas-tyey
Kindergarten	детский сад (m)	**dyet**-skeey saht
Lane	переулок (m)	pee-ree-**oo**-lak
Landscape	ландшафт (m),	lan-**shahft**,
	пейзаж (m)	peey-**zahsh**
Library	библиотека (f)	beeb-lee-a-**tye**-ka
Liquor store	винный магазин (m)	**veen**-niy ma-ga-**zeen**
Lost and found	бюро находок (n)	byoo-**ro** na-**kho**-dak
Market	рынок (m)	**ri**-nak

English	Russian	Pronunciation
Maternity-home	родильный дом (m)	ra-**deel'**-niy dom
Ministry	министерство (n)	mee-nees-**tyer**-stva
Mosque	мечеть (f)	mee-**chet'**
Motorcycle	мотоцикл (m)	ma-ta-**tsikl**
Mountain	гора (f)	ga-**rah**
Mountaineering	альпинизм (m)	al'-pee-**neezm**
Mountain range	горная цепь (f)	**gor**-na-ya tsep'
Museum	музей (m)	moo-**zyey**
Music center	музыкальный центр (m)	moo-zi-**kahl'**-niy tsentr
Music festival	фестиваль музыки (m)	fees-tee-**vahl'** **moo**-zi-kee
National park	национальный парк (m)	na-tsi-a-**nahl'**-niy pahrk
Nightclub	ночной клуб (m)	nach-**noy** kloop
Optician's-shop	магазин оптики (m)	ma-ga-**zeen** **op**-tee-kee

English	Russian	Pronunciation
Orphanage	сиротский дом (m)	see-**rot**-skeey dom
Park	парк (m)	pahrk
Pavilion	павильон (m)	pa-veel'-**on**
Pawnshop	ломбард (m)	lam-**bahrt**
Place of amusement	место развлечений (n)	**myes**-ta raz-vlee-**che**-neey
Plants	растения (pl.)	ras-**tye**-nee-ya
Poultry shop	магазин домашней птицы (m)	ma-ga-**zeen** da-**mahsh**-neey **ptee**-tsi
Real estate	недвижимость (f)	need-**vee**-zhi-mast'
Restaurant	ресторан (m)	rees-ta-**rahn**
Rickshaw	рикша (f)	**reek**-sha
River	река (f)	ree-**kah**
Road	дорога (f)	da-**ro**-ga
Rural-dispensary	сельский диспансер (m)	**syel's**-keey dees-pan-**ser**
School	школа (f)	**shko**-la
Scooter	скутер (m)	**skoo**-ter
Seafood	ресторан	rees-ta-**rahn**

English	Russian	Pronunciation
restaurant	продуктов моря (m)	pra-**dook**-taf **mo**-rya
Shoe shop	обувной	a-boov-**noy**
	магазин (m)	ma-ga-**zeen**
Shop	магазин (m)	ma-ga-**zeen**
Shopping mall	торговый центр (m)	tar-**go**-viy tsentr
Shop window	витрина (f)	veet-**ree**-na
Snackbar	буфет (m),	boo-**fyet** (m),
	закусочная (f)	za-**koo**-sach-na-ya (f)
Stadium	стадион (m)	sta-dee-**on**
Station	ста́нция (f)	**stahn**-tsi-ya
Stationer's	магазин	ma-ga-**zeen**
shop	канцтоваров (m)	**kahnts**-ta-**vah**-raf
Street	улица (f)	**oo**-lee-tsa
Street lamp	уличный	**oo**-leech-niy
	фонарь (m)	fa-**nahr'**
Street market	уличный рынок (m)	**oo**-leech-niy **ri**-nak
Swimming pool	бассейн (m)	ba-**syeyn**
Tailor's shop	портной (m)	part-**noy**
Taxi	такси (n)	tak-**see**

English	Russian	Pronunciation
Telephone	телефонная	tee-lee-**fon**-na-ya
booth	будка (f)	**boot**-ka
Temple	храм (m)	khrahm
Three wheeler	трехколесный	**tryokh**-ka-**lyos**-niy
	транспорт (m)	**trahns**-part
Ticket	билет (m)	bee-**lyet**
Tomb	могила (f)	ma-**gee**-la
Tower	башня (f)	**bahsh**-nya
Town	город (m)	**go**-rat
Toy shop	игрушечный	eeg-**roo**-shich-niy
	магазин (m)	ma-ga-**zeen**
Traffic	транспорт (m)	**trahns**-part
Traffic jam	(дорожная)	(da-**rozh**-na-ya)
	пробка (f)	**prop**-ka
Traffic lights	дорожные огни (pl.)	da-**rozh**-ni-ye ag-**nee**
Traffic sign	дорожный знак (m)	da-**rozh**-niy **znahk**
Train	поезд (m)	**po**-eest
Tram	трамвай (m)	tram-**vahy**

English	Russian	Pronunciation
Travel agency	бюро	byoo-**ro**
	путешествий (n)	poo-tee-**shest**-veey
Tree	дерево (n)	**dye**-ree-va
Truck	грузовик (m)	groo-za-**veek**
University	университет (m)	oo-nee-veer-see-**tyet**
Valley	долина (f)	da-**lee**-na
Village (small)	деревня (f)	dee-**ryev**-nya
Village (large)	село (n)	see-**lo**
Wall	стена (f)	stee-**nah**
Wall (city)	(городская)	(ga-rat-**skah**-ya)
	стена (f)	**stee**-na
Watchmaker's shop	часовня (f)	cha-**sov**-nya
Youth hostel	молодежный	ma-la-**dyozh**-niy
	хостел (m),	**khos**-tel,
	студенческое	stoo-**dyen**-chis-ka-ye
	общежитие (n)	ap-shchi-**zhi**-tee-ye

Do I need to book?

Я должен/должна забронировать?

Yah **dol**-zhin/dal-**zhnah** zab-ra-**nee**-ra-vat'?

I would like to confirm my ticket.

Я хочу подтвердить билет.

Yah kha-**choo** pat-tveer-**deet'** bee-**lyet**.

It's full.

Мест нет.

Myest nyet.

I would like to change my ticket.

Я хочу поменять билет.

Yah kha-**choo** pa-mee-**nyaht'** bee-**lyet**.

I would like to cancel my ticket.

Я хочу отменить билет.

Yah kha-**choo** at-mee-**neet'** bee-**lyet**.

Two tickets for the...tomorrow, please.

Два билета в... на завтра, пожалуйста.

Dvah bee-**lye**-ta v... na **zahf**-tra, pa-**zhah**-loos-ta.

Are children allowed?

Детям можно?

Dye-tyam **mozh**-na?

Two child's ticket, please.

Два детских билета, пожалуйста.

Dvah **dyet**-skeekh bee-**lye**-ta, pa-**zhah**-loos-ta.

Is transport included?

Транспорт включен?

Trahns-part vklyoo-**chon**?

Do I need to take food with me?

Мне нужно взять с собой еду?

Mnye **noozh**-na vzyaht' s sa-**boy** yee-**doo**?

Is lunch included?

Обед включен?

A-**byet** vklyoo-**chon**?

Everything included.

Все включено.

Vsyo vklyoo-chi-**no**.

I would like a guide book in English.

Я хочу путеводитель на английском.

Yah kha-**choo** poo-tee-va-**dee**-teel' na an-**gleey**-skam.

Do you have information on cultural sights?

У вас есть информация о культурных достопримечательных?

Oo vahs yest' een-far-**mah**-tsi-ya o kool'-**toor**-nih **dahs**-ta-pree-mee-**chah**-teel'-nas-tyakh?

I want to see local sights.

Я хочу посмотреть местные достопримечательности.

Yah kha-**choo** pas-mat-**ryet' myes**-ni-ye **dahs**-ta-pree-mee-**chah**-teel'-nas-tee.

Can we hire a guide?

Мы можем нанять гида?

Mi **mo**-zhim na-**nyaht' gee**-da?

Where do we meet?

Где встретимся?

Gdye **vstrye**-teem-sya?

When do we meet?

Когда встретимся?

Kag-**dah vstrye**-teem-sya?

When do we start off?
Когда отправляемся?
Kag-**dah** at-prav-**lyah**-yeem-sya?

Will we bee seeing the ... too?
Мы увидим... тоже?
Mi oo-**vee**-deem... **to**-zhe?

How much?
Сколько?
Skol'-ka?

The guide will pay.
Гид заплатит.
Geed zap-**lah**-teet.

When do we get back?
Когда мы вернемся?
Kag-**dah** mi veer-**nyom**-sya?

Can you recommend somewhere cheap but nice?
Вы можете посоветовать дешевое, но хорошее место?
Vi **mo**-zhi-tye pa-sa-**vye**-ta-vat' dee-**sho**-va-ye, no kha-**ro**-shi-ye **myes**-ta?

Can you recommend somewhere luxurious?

Вы можете посоветовать шикарное место?

Vi **mo**-zhi-tye pa-sa-**vye**-ta-vat' shi-**kahr**-na-ye **myes**-ta?

How long does the trip take?

Сколько длится поездка?

Skol'-ka **dleet**-sya pa-**yest**-ka?

When does... open?

Когда открывается...?

Kag-**dah** at-kri-**vah**-yeet-sya...?

When does... close?

Когда закрывается...?

Kag-**dah** zak-ri-**vah**-yeet-sya...?

Will we have some free time?

У нас будет свободное время?

Oo nahs **boo**-deet sva-**bod**-na-ye **vrye**-mya?

Will we be able to do some shopping?

Мы сможем сделать шопинг?

Mi **smo**-zhim **zdye**-lat' **sho**-peeng?

Can you recommend somewhere romantic?

Вы можете посоветовать романтическое место?

Vi **mo**-zhi-tye pa-sa-**vye**-ta-vaht' ra-man-**tee**-chis-ka-ye **myes**-ta?

What is the address?

Какой адрес?

Ka-**koy ad**-rees?

How long will we stay in... ?

Сколько мы пробудем в...?

Skol'-ka mi pra-**boo**-deem v...?

Is it long route?

Это долгий путь?

E-ta **dol**-geey poot'?

What's worth seeing in...?

Что стоит посмотреть в...?

Shto **sto**-eet pas-mat-**ryet'** v ...?

How much does the admission cost?

Сколько стоит вход?

Skol'-ka **sto**-eet fkhot?

The guide has paid.

Гид заплатил.

Geed zap-la-**teel.**

Is there an English speaking guide?

Здесь есть англоговорящий гид?

Zdyes' yest' **ahn**-gla-ga-va-**ryah**-shchiy geed?

I would like to see the... .

Я хочу посмотреть...

Yah kha-**choo** pas-mat-**ryet'**... .

Can we look at... today?

Мы можем взглянуть на... сегодня?

Mi **mo**-zhim vzglya-**noot'** na... see-**vod**-nya?

When does the tour start?

Когда начинается тур?

Kag-**dah** na-chi-**nah**-yeet-sya toor?

The tour includes two days in Saint-Petersburg.

Тур включает два дня в Санкт-Петербурге.

Toor vklyoo-**chah**-yeet dvah dnyah f Sahnkt-Pee-teer-**boor**-gye.

Can we take pictures?
Можно сфотографировать?
Mozh-na sfa-tag-ra-**fee**-ra-vat'?

What is this building/monument?
Что это за здание/памятник?
Shto **e**-ta za **zdah**-nee-ye/**pah**-meet-neek?

Who made it?
Кто сделал это?
Kto **zdye**-lal **e**-ta?

What time does it open/close?
Во сколько это открывается/закрывается?
Va **skol'**-ka **e**-ta at-kri-**vah**-yeet-sya/zak-ri-**vah**-yeet-sya?

What is the admission charge?
Сколько стоит вход?
Skol'-ka **sto**-eet fkhot?

Is there a discount for groups?
Для групп есть скидка?
Dlya groop yest' **skeet**-ka?

Who is the artist?
Кто художник?
Kto khoo-**dozh**-neek?

It is a painting of his early period.
Это картина его раннего периода.
E-ta kar-**tee**-na yee-**vo rahn**-nee-va pee-**ree**-a-da?

Which century does it belong to?
Каковoго это века?
Ka-**ko**-va **e**-ta **vye**-ka?

It dates from the 15th century.
Это 15-ого века.
E-ta 15-ava (pyat-**naht**-tsa-ta-va) **vye**-ka.

Could you take a photograph of me here?
Можете сфотографировать меня здесь?
Mo-zhi-tye sfa-tag-ra-**fee**-ra-vat' mee-**nyah** zdyes'?

Why is the museum closed?
Почему музей закрыт?
Pa-chi-**moo** moo-**zyey** zak-**rit**?

Is it a national heritage?

Это национальное наследие?

E-ta na-tsi-a-**nahl'**-na-ye nas-**lye**-dee-ye?

Where can I find?

Где я могу найти?

Gdye yah ma-**goo** nay-**tee**?

Where are the toilets?

Где туалет?

Gdye too-a-**lyet**?

We are just touring around.

Мы просто совершаем тур.

Mi **pros**-ta sa-veer-**shah**-yeem toor.

Is it a monument to Columbus?

Это памятник Колумбу?

E-ta **pah**-meet-neek Ka-**loom**-boo?

I am lost.

Я потерялся.

Yah pa-tee-**ryahl**-sya.

I have lost my group.

Я потерял свою группу.

Yah pa-tee-**ryahl** sva-**yoo groop**-poo.

Where is the nearest beach.

Где ближайший пляж?

Gdye blee-**zhahy**-shiy plyahsh?

Where is the nudist/best beach?

Где нудистский/самый лучший пляж?

Gdye noo-**deest**-skeey/**sah**-miy **looch**-shiy plyahsh?

Is it safe to dive/swim here?

Здесь безопасно нырять/плавать?

Zdyes' bee-za-**pahs**-na ni-**ryaht'**/**plah**-vat'?

How much is to rent a chair/an umbrella?

Сколько стоит взять на прокат стул/зонт?

Skol'-ka **sto**-eet vzyaht' na pra-**kaht** stool/zont?

When is the next daytrip?

Когда следующий тур?

Kag-**dah slye**-doo-shchiy toor?

Chapter-23

Directions

Направления (napravlyeneeya)

English	Russian	Pronunciation
Behind	за, сзади, позади	za, **zzah**-dee, pa- za-**dee**
East	восток (m)	vas-**tok**
Far away	далеко	da-lee-**ko**
Here	здесь	zdyes'
In front of	напротив	nap-**ro**-teef
Left	левый	**lye**-viy
Near	рядом	**ryah**-dam
Next to	рядом с	**ryah**-dam s
North	север (m)	**sye**-veer
North-East	северо-восток(m)	**sye**-vee-ra-vas-**tok**
North-West	северо-запад (m)	**sye**-vee-ra-**zah**-pat
Opposite	напротив, противоположный	nap-**ro**-teef, pra-tee-va-pa**lozh**-niy
Right	правый	**prah**-viy0
South	юг (m)	yook
South-East	юго-восток (m)	**yoo**-ga-vas-**tok**
South-West	юго-запад (m)	**yoo**-ga-**zah**-pat

English	Russian	Pronunciation
Straight ahead	прямо	**pryah**-ma
There	там	tahm
Turn (n)	поворот (m)	pa-va-**rot**
Turn left (v)	поворот налево	pa-va-**rot** na-**lye**-va
Turn right (v)	поворот направо	pa-va-**rot** na-**prah**-va
West	запад (m)	**zah**-pat

To face in direction...
Выходить в сторону...
Vi-kha-**deet'** f **sto**-ra-noo

Face this way!
Езжай этой дорогой!
Yeezh-**zhahy e**-tay da-**ro**-gay!

Turn at the corner.
Поверни на углу.
Pa-veer-**nee** na oog-**loo**.

Turn at the traffic lights.
Поверни у светофора.
Pa-veer-**nee** oo svee-ta-**fo**-ra.

Chapter-24

On the telephone
По телефону (pa tyeleefonoo)

Hello (making a call/answering a call)
Ало
A-**lo**

Is Mr. Pyetrov there?
Господина Петрова можно?
Gas-pa-**dee**-na Peet-**ro**-va **mozh**-na?

Can I speak to...?
Могу я поговорить с...?
Ma-**goo** yah pa-ga-va-**reet'** s...?

Speaking!
Это я!
E-ta yah!

Yes, I am Sasha. Tell me.
Да, это Саша. Слушаю.
Da, **e**-ta Sasha. **Sloo**-sha-yoo.

Who is calling, please?
Кто говорит, простите?
Kto ga-va-**reet**, pras-**tee**-tye?

Who do you want to speak to?
С кем вы хотите поговорить?
S kyem vi kha-**tee**-tye pa-ga-va-**reet'**?

Where are you calling from?
Откуда вы звоните?
At-**koo**-da vi zva-**nee**-tye?

I am calling from Moscow.
Я звоню из Москвы.
Yah zva-**nyoo** eez Mas-**kvi**.

You have the wrong number.
Не туда попали.
Nye too-**dah** pa-**pah**-lee.

What is your phone number?
Какой ваш номер телефона?
Ka-**koy** vahsh **no**-meer tee-lee-**fo**-na?

Could you put me through to Mr. Sidorov.

Соедините меня с господином Сидоровым.

Sa-yee-dee-**nee**-tye mee-**nyah** s gas-pah-**dee**-nam **Seed**-ra-vim.

Whose call is it?

Чей это звонок?

Chey **e**-ta zva-**nok**?

What number do you want?

Какой вам нужен номер?

Ka-**koy** vahm **noo**-zhen **no**-meer?

Can I take a message for him?

Можете оставить сообщение для него.

Mo-zhi-tye as-**tah**-veet' sa-ap-**shche**-nee-ye dlya nee-**vo**.

Please tell him I had called.

Пожалуйста, передайте ему, что я звонил(а).

Pa-**zhah**-loos-ta, pee-ree-**dahy**-tye yee-**moo**, shto yah zva-**neel**/zva-**nee**-la.

Could you give me the number of...?

Дайте мне номер... , пожалуйста.

Dahy-tye mnye **no**-meer..., pa-**zhah**-loos-ta.

Please speak after the tone.
Пожалуйста, говорите после сигнала.
Pa-**zhah**-loos-ta, ga-va-**ree**-tye **pos**-lee seeg-**nah**-la.

What is the code for India?
Какой код Индии?
Ka-**koy** kod **Een**-de-yee?

You omit '0' when dialing England from Russia.
Пропустите '0' когда звоните в Англию из России.
Pra-poos-**tee**-tye '0' kag-**dah** zva-**nee**-tye v **Ahn**-glee-yoo eez Ra-**see**-yee.

Would you repeat the number please?
Повторите, пожалуйста, номер.
Paf-ta-**ree**-tye, pa-**zhah**-loos-ta, **no**-meer.

Would you like to leave a message for him?
Хотите оставить сообщение для него?
Kha-**tee**-tye as-**tah**-veet' sa-ap-**shche**-nee-ye dlya nee-**vo**?

Can I dial direct to Delhi?
Я могу позвонить напрямую в Дели?
Yah ma-**goo** paz-va-**neet'** nap-rya-**moo**-yoo v **De**-lee?

You can dial the number direct.

Вы можете позвонить напрямую.

Vi **mo**-zhi-tye paz-va-**neet'** nap-rya-**moo**-yoo.

I want to make an international call.

Мне нужно сделать международный звонок.

Mnye **noozh**-na **zdye**-lat' meezh-doo-na-**rod**-niy zva-**nok**.

Would you give me an alarm call for 6.30 tomorrow morning please?

Разбудите меня, пожалуйста, в 6.30 утра завтра.

Raz-boo-**dee**-tye mee-**nyah**, pa-**zhah**-loos-ta, v 6.30 oot-**rah** **zahf**-tra.

There is no reply from...

Не отвечают из...

Nye at-vee-**chah**-yoot eez...

Please hold the line.

Оставайтесь на линии.

As-ta-**vahy**-tees' na **lee**-nee-yee.

The line is busy, I can't get through.

Линия занята, мне не дозвониться.

Lee-nee-ya za-nya-**tah**, mnye nye daz-va-**neet**-sya.

We have got a bad connection.

У нас плохое соединение.

Oo nahs pla-**kho**-ye sa-yee-dee-**nye**-nee-ye.

Please replace the receiver.

Замение трубку, пожалуйста.

Za-mee-**nee**-tye **troop**-koo, pa-**zhah**-loos-ta.

The phone is out of order.

Телефон не работает.

Tye-lee-**fon** nye ra-**bo**-ta-yeet.

Where is the nearest public phone?

Где ближайший таксофон?

Gdye blee-**zhahy**-sheey tak-sa-**fon**?

How much does a one minute call cost?

Сколько стоит одна минута разговора?

Skol'-ka **sto**-eet ad-**nah** mee-**noo**-ta raz-ga-**vo**-ra?

I need an adaptor plug.

Мне нужен переходник.

Mnye **noo**-zhin pee-ree-khad-**neek**.

I have lost the charger for my phone.

Я потерял(а) зарядку для телефона.

Yah pa-tee-**ryahl**/pa-tee-**ryah**-la za-**ryaht**-koo dlya tye-lee-**fo**-na.

I want a mobile/cell phone for hire for a week.

Я хочу взять телефон на неделю.

Yah kha-**choo** vzyaht' tee-lee-**fon** na nee-**dye**-lyoo.

Do you have prepaid phone?

У вас есть pre-paid тариф?

Oo vahs yest' pre-paid ta-**reef**?

This is not the SIM card for your network.

Это сим-карта не вашей сети.

E-ta seem-**kahr**-ta nye **vah**-shey see-**tee**.

Chapter-25

Customs
Таможня (tamozhnya)

Can I see your passport, please.
Покажите паспорт, пожалуйста.
Pa-ka-**zhi**-tye **pahs**-part, pa-**zhah**-loos-ta.

Do I have anything to declare?
Мне нужно что-нибудь задекларировать?
Mnye **noozh**-na **shto**-nee-boot' za-deek-la-**ree**-ra-vat'?

I have articles of my personal use.
У меня есть личные вещи.
Oo mee-**nyah** yest' **leech**-ni-ye **vye**-shchi.

That isn't mine.
Это не мое.
E-ta nye ma-**yo**.

Please open!
Откройте, пожалуйста!
At-**kroy**-tye, pa-**zhah**-loos-ta!

This is a present.
Это подарок.
E-ta pa-**dah**-rak.

I have cigarettes.
У меня есть сигареты.
Oo mee-**nyah** yest' see-ga-**rye**-ti.

That's my suitcase.
Это мой чемодан.
E-ta moy chi-ma-**dahn**.

Do I have to pay duty on...?
Мне нужно заплатить налог на...?
Mnye **noozh**-na zap-la-**teet'** na-**lok** na...?

It's a bottle of perfume.
Это духи.
E-ta doo-**khee**.

It belongs to me.
Это мое.
E-ta ma-**yo**.

Chapter-26

At the restaurant
В ресторане (v reestarahnye)

Which local dishes do you recommend?
Какие местные блюда вы рекомендуете?
Ka-**kee**-ye **myes**-ni-ye **blyoo**-da vi ree-ka-meen-**doo**-yee-te?

Is there a good Chinese restaurant here?
Здесь есть хороший китайский ресторан?
Zdyes' yest' kha-**ro**-sheey kee-**tahys**-keey rees-ta-**rahn**?

Which restaurant is the cheapest here?
Какой здесь самый дешевый ресторан?
Ka-**koy** zdyes' **sah**-miy dee-**sho**-viy rees-ta-**rahn**?

Is there a vegetarian restaurant here?
Здесь есть вегетарианский ресторан?
Zdyes' yest' vee-gee-ta-ree-**ahn**-skeey rees-ta-**rahn**?

I would like to reserve a table for three people.
Я хочу заказать стол на троих.
Yah kha-**choo** za-ka-**zaht'** stol na tra-**eekh**.

Are you still serving food?
Вы еще работаете?
Vi yee-**shcho** ra-**bo**-ta-yee-te?

Where would you like to sit?
Где вы хотите сесть?
Gdye vi kha-**tee**-tye syest'?

Is it self-service?
Здесь самообслуживание?
Zdyes' **sah**-ma-aps-**loo**-zhi-va-nee-ye?

Waiter!/Waitress!
Официант!
A-fee-**tsahnt**!

Have you ordered?
Вы заказали?
Vi za-ka-**zah**-lee?

Would you like a drink while you wait?
Хотите напиток во время ожидания?
Kha-**tee**-tye na-**pee**-tak vo **vrye**-mya a-zhi-**dah**-nee-ya?

What is the menu?
Какое меню?
Ka-**ko**-ye mee-**nyoo**?

I would like to taste a local speciality.
Я хочу попробовать местное фирменное блюдо.
Yah kha-**choo** pa-**pro**-ba-vat' **myes**-na-ye **feer**-mee-na-ye **blyoo**-da.

Do you have a menu in English?
У вас есть меню на английском?
Oo vahs yest' mee-**nyoo** na an-**gleey**-skam?

Do you have children's meals?
У вас есть блюда для детей?
Oo vahs yest' **blyoo**-da dlya dee-**tyey**?

Is there a baby change room?
Здесь есть комната для детей?
Zdyes' yest' **kom**-na-ta dlya dee-**tyey**?

Is there a high chair?
Здесь есть высокий стул?
Zdyes' yest' vi-**so**-keey stool?

Is there family discount?

Здесь есть семейная скидка?

Zdyes' yest' see-**myey**-na-ya **skeet**-ka?

I would like to see a drink-list.

Я хочу посмотреть меню напитков.

Yah kha-**choo** pas-mat-**ryet'** mee-**nyoo** na-**peet**-kaf.

We only want drinks.

Мы хотим только напитки.

Mi kha-**teem tol'**-ka na-**peet**-kee.

Please bring a glass.

Принесите стакан, пожалуйста.

Pree-nee-**see**-tye sta-**kahn**, pa-**zhah**-loos-ta.

Please bring a serviette/ a wineglass.

Принесите салфетку/бокал для вина, пожалуйста.

Pree-nee-**see**-tye sal-**fyet**-koo/ba-**kahl** dlya vee-**nah**, pa-**zhah**-loos-ta.

How long is the wait?

Как долго ждать?

Kak **dol**-ga zhdaht'?

What shall we start off with?
С чего нам начать?
S chee-**vo** nahm na-**chaht'**?

Is this seat taken?
Это место занято?
E-ta **myes**-ta **zah**-nya-ta?

Would you like a drink, sir?
Напиток, сэр?
Na-**pee**-tak, ser?

Some water, please.
Воду, пожалуйста.
Vo-doo, pa-**zhah**-loos-ta.

Yes, I would like to have...
Да, я хочу...
Da, yah kha-**choo**...

I'm on a ... diet.
Я на ... диете.
Yah na ... dee-**ye**-tye.

I don't eat any meat.

Я не ем мяса.

Yah nye yem **myah**-sa.

Could I have some of that cheese.

Можно мне того сыра.

Mozh-na mnye ta-**vo si**-ra.

I really couldn't.

Я, правда, не могу.

Yah, **prahv**-da, nye ma-**goo**.

It is fresh from the oven.

Это только из духовки.

E-ta **tol'**-ka eez doo-**khof**-kee.

Is it cooked with butter?

Это с маслом?

E-ta s **mahs**-lam?

Is it cooked in butter?

Это приготовлено на масле?

E-ta pree-ga-**tov**-lee-na na **mahs**-lye?

I will check with the cook.
Я уточню у повара.
Yah oo-tach-**nyoo** oo **po**-va-ra.

What would you recommend?
Что вы порекомендуете?
Shto vi pa-ree-ka-meen-**doo**-yee-tye?

Could you prepare a meal without eggs/meat/fish?
Вы можете приготовить блюдо без яиц/мяса/рыбы?
Vi **mo**-zhi-tye pree-ga-**to**-veet' **blyoo**-da byez ya-**eets**/**myah**-sa/**ri**-bi?

I don't want it deep-fried.
Я не хочу очень жареное.
Yah nee kha-**choo** **o**-cheen' **zhah**-ree-na-ye.

I would like it steamed.
Я хочу (блюдо) на пару.
Yah kha-**choo** (**blyoo**-da) na pa-**roo**.

I would like it with the dressing on the side.
Я хочу с соусом отдельно.
Yah kha-**choo** s **so**-oo-sam ad-**dyel'**-na.

Does it take long to prepare?
Это долго готовить?
E-ta **dol**-ga ga-**to**-veet'?

What is in that dish?
Из чего состоит это блюдо?
Ees chee-**vo** sas-ta-**yeet e**-ta **blyoo**-da?

Is this free of animal produce?
Это вегетарианское?
E-ta vee-gee-ta-ree-**ahn**-ska-ye?

A pot of coffee for two.
Чайник кофе на двоих.
Chahy-neek **ko**-fe na dva-**eekh**.

I like my meat well done.
Я хочу хорошо приготовленное блюдо.
Yah kha-**choo** kha-ra-**sho** pree-ga-**tov**-leen-na-yé **blyoo**-da.

Help yourself!
Угощайтесь!
Oo-ga-**shchahy**-tees'!

They treated to him to a dinner.

Они угостили его за ужином.

A-**nee** oo-gas-**tee**-lee yee-**vo** za **oo**-zhi-nam.

It's my treat.

Я угощаю.

Yah oo-ga-**shchah**-yoo.

Have you tried these...

Вы пробовали эти...

Vi **pro**-ba-va-le **e**-tee...

I love this dish.

Мне очень нравится это блюдо.

Mnye **o**-cheen' **nrah**-veet-sya **e**-ta **blyoo**-da.

This is burnt/too cold.

Подгорело/остыло.

Pad-ga-**rye**-la/as-**ti**-la.

This is superb.

тлично.

At-**leech**-na.

My bill. please.

Счет, пожалуйста.

Shchot, pa-**zhah**-loos-ta.

Could we have separate bills.

Рассчитайте нас по отдельности.

Ras-shchi-**tahy**-tyè nahs po ad-**dyel'**-nas-tee.

May I have a dance with you?

Могу я пригласить вас на танец?

Ma-**goo** yah preeg-la-**seet'** vahs na **tah**-neets?

Sorry I can't dance.

Извините, я не танцую.

Eez-vee-**nee**-tye, yah nye tan-**tsoo**-yoo.

Will you have some more?

Добавки?

Da-**bahf**-kee?

Ice cream with a banana flavour.

Банановое мороженое.

Ba-**nah**-na-va-ye ma-**ro**-zhi-na-ye.

Should I add milk in your coffee?
Вам добавить молока в кофе?
Vahm da-**bah**-veet' ma-la-**kah** f **ko**-fe?

I want to have a cigarette. May I?
Я хочу покурить. Можно?
Yah kha-**choo** pa-koo-**reet'**. **Mozh**-na?

You may/may not smoke.
Можете курить./ Курить нельзя.
Mo-zhi-tye koo-**reet'**./ Koo-**reet'** neel'-**zyah**.

Is service included in the bill?
Сервис входит в счет?
Syer-vees **fkho**-deet f shchot?

10% service is included.
10% за сервис включены.
Dye-syat' pra-**tsen**-taf za **syer**-vees fklyoo-chi-**ni**.

You have billed me for... euros instead of... .
Вы посчитали ... евро вместо... .
Vi pas-shchee-**tah**-lee... **yev**-ro **vmyes**-ta... .

We love the local cuisine.

Мы любим местную кухню.

Mi **lyoo**-beem **myes**-noo-yoo **kookh**-nyoo.

That was delicious!

Это было очень вкусно!

E-ta **bi**-la **o**-cheen' **fkoos**-na!

Chapter-27

At the Bar
В баре (v bahrye)

A double whisky.
Двойной виски.
Dvay-**noy** **vees**-kee.

Cheers!
Чиас!
Chee-as!

Do you like soda with it?
Хотите добавить соду?
Kha-**tee**-tye da-**bah**-veet' **so**-doo?

Do you serve meals here?
Здесь есть кухня?
Zdyes' yest' **kookh**-nya?

Excuse me!
Извините!
Eez-vee-**nee**-tye!

Here's to you.
Это вам.
E-ta vahm.

How much is that?
Сколько это стоит?
Skol'-ka **e**-ta **sto**-yeet?

I am feeling drunk.
Я пьян/пьяна.
Yah pyahn/pya-**nah**.

I am next.
Потом я.
Pa-**tom** yah.

I prefer gin and soda.
Я предпочитаю джин с содой.
Yah preet-pa-chi-**tah**-yoo dzhin s **so**-day.

I think I have had too many.
Думаю, мне достаточно.
Doo-ma-yoo, mnye das-**tah**-tach-na.

It's my round.
Моя очередь.
Ma-**yah o**-chi-reet'.

I will buy you a drink.
Я куплю тебе выпить.
Yah koop-**lyoo** tee-**bye vi**-peet'.

Let me treat you to a drink.
Позволь мне пригласить вас выпить.
Paz-**vol'**-tye mnye preeg-la-**seet'** vahs **vi**-peet'.

No ice, thanks.
Лед не надо, спасибо.
Lyot nee **nah**-da, spa-**see**-ba.

Round of drinks, please.
По рюмочке для всех, пожалуйста.
Po **ryoo**-mach-kye dlya vsyekh, pa-**zhah**-loos-ta.

Same again, please.
Повторите, пожалуйста.
Paf-ta-**ree**-tye, pa-**zhah**-loos-ta.

Thanks, but I don't feel like it.
Спасибо, но мне не хочется.
Spa-**see**-ba, no mnye nye **kho**-cheet-sya.

The wine is extra.
Еще вина.
Yee-**shcho** vee-**nah**.

This drink is 40% proof.
В этом напитке 40 градусов.
V **e**-tam na-**peet**-kye 40 (**so**-rak) **grah**-doo-saf.

This is hitting the spot.
Это то, что надо.
E-ta to, shto **nah**-da.

We drink it straight.
Мы пьем не смешивая.
Mi pyom nye **smye**-shi-va-ya.

Will you have a drink?
Выпьешь?
Vi-p'yesh?

Whisky with a splash of water, please.
Виски с капелькой воды, пожалуйста.
Vees-kee s **kah**-peel'-koy va-**di**, pa-**zhah**-loos-ta.

You can get the next one.
Вы можете взять еще один.
Vi **mo**-zhi-tye vzyaht' yee-**shcho** a-**deen**.

Chapter-28

At the Hotel
В гостинице (v gasteeneetse)

Do you have any accommodation available?

У вас есть свободные комнаты?

Oo vahs yest' sva-**bod**-ni-ye **kom**-na-ti?

I would like to book a room, please.

Я хочу заказать номер, пожалуйста.

Yah kha-**choo** za-ka-**zaht' no**-meer, pa-**zhah**-loos-ta.

How much is it per night/week for a person?

Сколько стоит одна ночь/неделя на человека?

Skol'-ka **sto**-yeet ad-**nah** noch/nee-**dye**-lya na chee-la-**vye**-ka?

I already tried 2 hotels but they had no room.

Я уже спросил в двух гостиницах, но там нет комнат.

Yah oo-**zhe** spra-**seel** v dvookh gas-**tee**-nee-tsakh, no tahm nyet **kom**-nat.

I have a reservation.
У меня резервация.
Oo mee-**nyah** ree-zeer-**vah**-tsi-ya.

Sorry we are full up for/till...
Извините, у нас все занято на/до...
Eez-vee-**nee**-tye, oo nahs vsyo **zah**-nee-ta na/do...

The hotel is booked up.
Отель зарезервирован.
A-**tel'** za-ree-zeer-**veer**-ra-van.

Please book us in for Sunday.
Пожалуйста, забронируйте для нас на воскресенье.
Pa-**zhah**-loos-ta, za-bra-**nee**-rooy-tye dlya nahs na vas-kree-**syen'**-ye.

For two nights.
На две ночи.
Na dvye **no**-chi.

Single room or double room?
Комната на одного или на двоих?
Kom-na-ta na ad-na-**vo ee**-lee na dva-**eekh**?

A.c. or non a.c.?

С кондиционером или без?

S kan-dee-tsi-a-**nye**-ram **ee**-lee byes?

I would prefer a single/double a.c./non a.c. room.

Я предпочитаю одноместную/двухместную комнату с кондиционером/без кондиционера.

Yah preet-pa-chi-**tah**-yoo ad-na-**myes**-noo-yoo/dvookh-**myes**-noo-yoo **kom**-na-too s kan-dee-tsi-a-**nye**-ram/byes kan-dee-tsi-a-**nye**-ra.

For how many nights?

На сколько ночей?

Na **skol'**-ka na-**chey**?

Yes, please check in here.

Да, зарегистрируйтесь здесь, пожалуйста.

Da, za-ree-gee-**stree**-rooy-tyes' zdyes', pa-**zhah**-loos-ta.

I would prefer the top/ground/first floor, please.

Я предпочитаю верхний/нижний/второй этаж, пожалуйста.

Yah preet-pa-chi-**tah**-yoo **vyerkh**-neey/**neezh**-neey/fta-**roy** ee-**tahzh**, pa-**zhah**-loos-ta.

What is the check-out time?
Во сколько чек-аут?
Va **skol'**-ka **chek**-**ah**-oot?

How much extra to stay until 9 o'clock?
Сколько надо доплатить до 9 утра?
Skol'-ka **nah**-da dap-la-**teet'** do 9 (dee-vee-**tee**) oot-**rah**?

Can I checkout late?
Можно я уеду поздно?
Mozh-na yah oo-**ye**-doo **poz**-na?

Can I see it?
Можно посмотреть?
Mozh-na pas-mat-**ryet'**?

It's fine, I'll take it.
Хорошо, я беру.
Kha-ra-**sho**, yah bee-**roo**.

Can I pay by credit card/traveler's check?
Можно оплатить кредитной картой/дорожным чеком?
Mozh-na ap-la-**teet'** kree-**deet**-nay **kahr**-toy/da-**rozh**-nim **che**-kam?

Which is the room assigned to me?
Где моя комната?
Gdye ma-**yah** **kom**-na-ta?

Is there a safe in this hotel?
В этой гостинице есть сейф?
V **e**-tay gas-**tee**-nee-tse yest' syeyf?

It's a service that has to be paid for.
Это платная услуга.
E-ta **plaht**-na-ya oos-**loo**-ga.

You have to add... euros on for service.
Вы должны добавить... евро за сервис.
Vi dalzh-**ni** da-**bah**-veet' ... **yev**-ra za **syer**-vees.

With the compliments of the management.
С наилучшими пожеланиями от администрации.
S na-ee-**looch**-shi-mee pa-zhi-**lah**-nee-ya-mee ot ad-mee-nee-**strah**-tsi-yee.

Is there a room reserved for wife and self?
Здесь есть комната, заказанная для меня с женой?
Zdyes' yest' **kom**-na-ta, za-**kah**-za-na-ya dlya mee-**nyah** s zhi-**noy**?

Sorry, but the service is poor in this hotel.
Извините, но сервис в отеле плохой.
Eez-vee-**nee**-tye, no **syer**-vees v a-**te**-lye pla-**khoy**.

Is service included in the bill?
Сервис включен в счет?
Syer-vees vklyoo-**chon** f shchot?

Yes, 10% service is included.
Да, 10% за сервис включены.
Da, 10% (**dye**-seet' pra-**tsen**-taf) za **syer**-vees vklyoo-chi-**ni**.

Can I leave my bags here?
Я могу оставить здесь сумки?
Yah ma-**goo** as-**tah**-veet' zdyes' **soom**-kee?

Is there a swimming pool?
Здесь есть бассейн?
Zdyes' yest' bas-**syeyn**?

Who is it?
Кто это?
Kto **e**-ta?

Room service, please.
Комнатное обслуживание, пожалуйста.
Kom-nat-na-ye aps-**loo**-zhi-va-nee-ye, pa-**zhah**-loos-ta.

Just a moment.
Одну минуту.
Ad-**noo** mee-**noo**-too.

Come in!
Входите!
Fkha-**dee**-tye!

I am at your service.
Я к вашим услугам.
Yah k **vah**-shim oos-**loo**-gam.

Could you come back later, please.
Вы можете прийти попозже, пожалуйста.
Vi **mo**-zhi-tye preey-**tee** pa-**pozh**-zhe, pa-**zhah**-loos-ta.

Did you call, sir/madam?
Вы вызывали, сэр/мадам?
Vi vi-zi-**vah**-lee, ser/ma-**dahm**?

Please wake me at seven.

Пожалуйста, разбудите меня в семь.

Pa-**zhah**-loos-ta, raz-boo-**dee**-tye mee-**nyah** f syem'.

Is there any message for me?

Для меня есть сообщение?

Dlya mee-**nyah** yest' sa-ap-**shche**-nee-ye?

Is there any post/parcel for me?

Для меня есть письмо/посылка?

Dlya mee-**nyah** yest' pees'-**mo**/pa-**sil**-ka?

There is a parcel/letter for you.

Для вас посылка/письмо.

Dlya vahs pa-**sil**-ka/pees'-**mo**.

From where did it come?

Откуда это пришло?

At-**koo**-da **e**-ta preesh-**lo**?

It came with the post.

Пришло по почте.

Preesh-**lo** po **poch**-tye.

When did it come?
Когда это пришло?
Kag-**dah e**-ta preesh-**lo**?

It came this morning.
Это пришло утром.
E-ta preesh-**lo oot**-ram.

There is a parcel/letter addressed to Mr. Ivanov.
Здесь посылка/письмо для мистера Иванова.
Zdyes' pa-**sil**-ka/pees'-**mo** dlya **mees**-te-ra Ee-va-**no**-va.

When/Where's breakfast served?
Когда/Где подают завтрак?
Kag-**dah**/Gdye pa-da-**yoot zahf**-trak?

Can I use laundry?
Я могу использовать прачечную?
Yah ma-**goo** ees-**pol'**-za-vat' **prah**-chich-noo-yoo?

Do you also arrange tours?
Вы устраиваете туры?
Vi oos-**trah**-ee-va-yee-tye **too**-ri?

Can you call a taxi for me?

Вы можете вызвать мне такси?

Vi **mo**-zhi-tye **viz**-vat' mnye tak-**see**?

Can I use your telephone?

Можно воспользоваться вашим телефоном?

Mozh-na vas-**pol'**-za-vat-sya **vah**-sheem tee-lee-**fo**-nam?

I am leaving now.

Я уезжаю сейчас.

Yah oo-yeezh-**zhah**-yoo see-**chahs**.

Could I have my deposit please?

Можно мне мой депозит?

Mozh-na mnye moy dee-pa-**zeet**?

Did you have a pleasant stay?

Вам понравилось место?

Vahm pan-**rah**-vee-las' **myes**-ta?

Yes!

Да!

Dah!

Chapter-29

Complaints
Жалобы (zhalabi)

The shower doesn't work.

Душ не работает.

Doosh nye ra-**bo**-ta-yeet.

Light doesn't work.

Света нет.

Svye-ta nyet.

We will check it too.

Мы это тоже проверим.

Mi **e**-ta **to**-zhe pra-**vye**-reem.

The door of my room no.202 doesn't close properly.

Дверь моей комнаты номер 202 нормально не закрывается.

Dvyer' ma-**yey** **kom**-na-ti **no**-meer 202 (**dvyes**-tee dvah) nar-**mahl'**-na nye zak-ri-**vah**-yeet-sya.

Please have it prepared

Подготовьте, пожалуйста.

Pad-ga-**tof'**-tye, pa-**zhah**-loos-ta.

The window doesn't open/close.

Окно не открывается/закрывается.

Ak-**no** nye at-kri-**vah**-yeet-sya/zak-ri-**vah**-yeet-sya.

The lift is stuck at the seventh floor.

Лифт застрял на седьмом этаже.

Leeft zas-**tryahl** na seed'-**mom** e-ta-**zhe**.

I am locked out of my room.

Моя дверь захлопнулась.

Ma-**yah** dvyer' za-**khlop**-noo-las'.

The air-conditioning/fan doesn't work.

Кондиционер/вентилятор не работает.

Kan-dee-tsi-a-**nyer**/veen-tee-**lyah**-tar nye ra-**bo**-ta-yeet.

The toilet is not clean.

В туалете грязно.

F too-a-**lye**-tye **gryahz**-na.

There is a cockroach in the bathroom.

В ванной таракан.

V **vahn**-nay ta-ra-**kahn**.

The bathroom is locked.

Ванная закрыта.

Vahn-na-ya zak-**ri**-ta.

The room is too dark.

Эта комната слишком темная.

E-ta **kom**-na-ta **sleesh**-kam **tyom**-na-ya.

The sheets are not clean.

Простыни грязные.

Pros-ti-nee **gryahz**-ni-ye.

The room is too cold/small.

Эта комната слишком холодная/маленькая.

E-ta **kom**-na-ta **sleesh**-kam kha-**lod**-na-ya/**mah**-leen'-ka-ya.

Chapter-30

Asking the Way

Как пройти... (kahk pray<u>tee</u>)

Am I right for the airport?
Я правильно еду к аэропорту?
Yah **prah**-veel'-na **ye**-doo k a-ee-ra-**por**-too?

Are we on the right way?
Мы правильно едем?
Mi **prah**-veel'-na **ye**-deem?

Can I give you a lift for the airport?
Могу я подвести вас к аэропорту?
Ma-**goo** yah pad-vees-**tee** vahs k a-ee-ra-**por**-too?

Can you direct me to the market?
Как пройти к рынку?
Kak pray-**tee** k **rin**-koo?

How can we go to the shortest way to the monument?
Где кратчайший путь до памятника?
Gdye krat-**chahy**-sheey poot' do **pah**-meet-nee-ka?

How far is it to the airport?

Как далеко до аэропорта?

Kak da-lee-**ko** do a-ee-ra-**por**-ta?

It's a long drive.

Долгая дорога.

Dol-ga-yah da-**ro**-ga.

It's a short car run.

На машине недалеко.

Na ma-**shi**-nye nee-da-lee-**ko**.

It's two blocks away.

Это через два квартала.

E-ta **che**-reez dvah kvar-**tah**-la.

Is this the right place?

Это то самое место?

E-ta **to sah**-ma-ye **myes**-ta?

Is this the road for...?

Это дорога к...?

E-ta da-**ro**-ga k...?

Is it far?

Это далеко?

E-ta da-lee-**ko**?

It is on the other side of the street.

Это на другой стороне улицы.

E-ta na droo-**goy** sta-ra-**nye** **oo**-lee-tsi.

It is in the direction of...

Это в сторону...

E-ta f **sto**-ra-noo...

It is 10 kilometers to the palace.

До дворца 10 километров.

Do dvar-**tsah** 10 (**dye**-seet') kee-la-**myet**-raf.

This isn't the way to...

Эта дорога не ведет к...

E-ta da-**ro**-ga nye vee-**dyot** k...

This road leads back to the hotel.

Эта дорога ведет обратно к отелю.

E-ta da-**ro**-ga vee-**dyot** ab-**raht**-na k a-**te**-lyoo.

This road meets up with the motorway.

Эта дорога соединяется с магистралью.

E-ta da-**ro**-ga sa-yee-dee-**nyah**-yeet-sya s ma-gees-**trahl'**-yoo.

This street leads to...

Эта улица ведет к...

E-ta **oo**-lee-tsa vee-**dyot** k...

Take the first on the right.

Сверните на первом повороте направо.

Sveer-**nee**-tye na **pyer**-vam pa-va-**ro**-tye nap-**rah**-va.

We take the road to...

Мы поедем к...

Mi pa-**ye**-deem k...

We have a long way to go.

Нам далеко ехать.

Nam da-lee-**ko** **ye**-khat'.

Where are you bound for?

Куда вам нужно?

Koo-**dah** vahm **noozh**-na?

Where do we go from here?
Куда мы выедем отсюда?
Koo-**dah** mi **vi**-yee-deem at-**syoo**-da?

Where does this road lead?
Куда ведет эта дорога?
Koo-**dah** vee-**dyot** **e**-ta da-**ro**-ga?

Can you show me on the map?
Можете показать на карте?
Mo-zhi-tye pa-ka-**zaht'** na **kahr**-tye?

Which is the way to the station, please?
Простите, как доехать до станции?
Pras-**tee**-tye, kak da-**ye**-khat' do **stahn**-tsi-ee?

Which way to the airport?
Какая дорога ведет к аэропорту?
Ka-**kah**-ya da-**ro**-ga vee-**dyot** k a-ee-ra-**por**-too?

You are a long way out.
Вы далеко от правильного пути.
Vi da-lee-**ko** ot **prah**-veel'-na-va poo-**tee**.

Chapter-31

Taxi
Такси (taksee)

Is this taxi free?
Это такси свободно?
E-ta tak-**see** sva-**bod**-na?

Please put the meter on.
Включите счетчик, пожалуйста.
Vklyoo-**chi**-tye **shchot**-chik, pa-**zhah**-loos-ta.

How much is it to...?
Сколько стоит до...?
Skol'-ka **sto**-eet do...?

Please take me to this address.
Отвезите меня по этому адресу, пожалуйста.
At-vee-**zee**-tye mee-**nyah** po **e**-ta-moo **ahd**-ree-soo, pa-**zhah**-loos-ta.

How much is the final fare?
Какая последняя цена?
Ka-**kah**-ya pas-**lyed**-nya-ya tse-**nah**?

Please slow down.
Помедленнее, пожалуйста.
Pa-**myed**-leen-nee-ye, pa-**zhah**-loos-ta.

Please wait here.
Подождите здесь, пожалуйста.
Pa-dazh-**dee**-tye zdyes', pa-**zhah**-loos-ta.

Stop at the corner.
Остановитесь на углу.
As-ta-na-**vee**-tyes' na oog-**loo**.

Chapter-32

In the Police Station
В полиции (f paleetsiyee)

I would like to report a theft.
Я хочу сообщить о краже.
Yah kha-**choo** sa-ap-**shchit'** o **krah**-zhi.

I have lost my passport/purse.
Я потерял/потеряла паспорт/кошелек.
Yah pa-tee-**ryahl**/pa-tee-**ryah**-la **pahs**-part/ka-shi-**lyok**.

I have been robed.
Меня обокрали.
Mee-**nyah** a-bak-**rah**-lee.

I am not guilty.
Я не виновен/виновна.
Yah nye vee-**no**-veen/vee-**nov**-na.

I want to contact my embassy/consulate.
Я хочу связаться со своим посольством/консульством.
Yah kha-**choo** svee-**zaht**-sya so sva-**yeem** pa-**sol'**-stvam/**kon**-sool'-stvam.

I need a lawyer who speaks English.

Мне нужен англо-говорящий адвкокат.

Mnye **noo**-zhin **ahn**-gla-ga-va-**ryah**-sheey ad-va-**kaht**.

It's not my fault.

Это не моя вина.

E-ta nye ma-**yah** vee-**nah**.

I apologize.

Я прошу прощения.

Yah pra-**shoo** pra-**shche**-nee-ya.

Can I pay an on-the-spot fine?

Могу я заплатить немедленный штраф?

Ma-**goo** yah zap-la-**teet'** nee-**myed**-leen-niy shtrahf?

Chapter-33

In the Bank
В банке (v bahnkye)

Where can I...?
Где я могу...?
Gdye yah ma-**goo**...?

I would like to cash a cheque.
Я хочу обналичить чек.
Yah kha-**choo** ab-na-**lee**-chit' chek.

I would like to change money.
Я хочу поменять деньги.
Yah kha-**choo** pa-mee-**nyaht' dyen'**-gee.

What time does the bank open?
Во сколько открывается банк?
Va **skol'**-ka at-kri-**vah**-yeet-sya bahnk?

Can I arrange a transfer?
Могу я сделать перевод?
Ma-**goo** yah **zdye**-lat' pee-ree-**vot**?

I have forgotten my pin no.

Я забыл/забыла свой пин-код.

Yah za-**bil**/za-**bi**-la svoy peen-**kot**.

What is the exchange rate?

Какой курс?

Ka-**koy** koors?

Can I see your passport, please.

Покажите паспорт, пожалуйста.

Pa-ka-**zhi**-tye **pahs**-part, pa-**zhah**-loos-ta.

Chapter-34

At the Border
На границе (na graneetse)

Your passport, please.
Ваш паспорт, пожалуйста.
Vahsh **pahs**-part, pa-**zhah**-loos-ta.

Your visa, please.
Вашу визу, пожалуйста.
Vah-shoo **vee**-zoo, pa-**zhah**-loos-ta.

Are you travelling in a group/with family?
Вы путешествуете с группой/с семьей?
Vi poo-tee-**shes**-tvoo-yee-tye z **groop**-poy/s seem'-**yoy**?

Are you travelling on your own?
Вы путешествуете один/одна?
Vi poo-tee-**shest**-voo-yee-tye a-**deen**/ad-**nah**?

Your papers, please.
Ваши документы, пожалуйста.
Vah-shi da-koo-**myen**-ti, pa-**zhah**-loos-ta.

What is purpose of visit?
Какова цель вашего визита?
Ka-ka-**vah** tsel' **vah**-shi-va vee-**zee**-ta?

I am on business here.
Я здесь по делам.
Yah zdyes' po dee-**lahm**.

I am here on holiday.
Я здесь на выходных.
Yah zdyes' na vi-khad-**nih**.

I am here for 2 days/1 month.
Я здесь на 2 дня/1 месяц.
Yah zdyes' na 2 (dvah) dnyah/1 (a-**deen**) **mye**-seets.

I am here for 2 weeks.
Я здесь на 2 недели.
Yah zdyes' na 2 (dvye) nee-**dye**-lee.

I have nothing to declare.
Мне нечего декларировать.
Mnye **nye**-chi-va deek-la-**ree**-ra-vat'.

Chapter-35

Socializing

Общение (apshcheneeye)

Are you free tomorrow?
Ты занят/занята завтра?
Ti **zah**-nyat/za-nya-**tah zahf**-tra?

What are you doing this evening?
Что ты делаешь сегодня вечером?
Shto ti **dye**-la-yeesh see-**vod**-nya **vye**-chee-ram?

What are you doing now?
Что ты сейчас делаешь?
Shto ti see-**chahs dye**-la-yeesh?

Would you like to go for a meal/drink?
Не хочешь пойти поесть/выпить?
Nye **kho**-cheesh pay-**tee** pa-**yest'**/**vi**-peet'?

Can you come to dinner?
Придешь на ужин?
Pree-**dyosh** na **oo**-zhin?

I will pick you up.
Я зайду за тобой.
Yah **zahy**-doo za ta-**boy**.

Are you ready?
Ты готов/готова?
Ti ga-**tof**/ga-**to**-va?

Yes, I am ready.
Да, я готов/готова.
Dah, yah ga-**tof**/ga-**to**-va.

Let me treat you to a drink.
Позволь мне пригласить тебя выпить.
Paz-**vol'** mnye preeg-la-**seet'** tee-**byah vi**-peet'.

Will you join me in a drink?
Выпьешь со мной?
Vip'-yesh so mnoy?

Would you like to go for a walk?
Хочешь прогуляться?
Kho-chish pra-goo-**lyaht**-sya?

May I join you?
Я присоединюсь к вам?
Yah pree-sa-yee-dee-**nyoos'** k vahm?

Ok!
Окей!
O-kyey!

I feel like going out somewhere.
Мне хочется сходить куда-нибудь.
Mnye **kho**-cheet-sya skha-**deet'** koo-**dah**-nee-**boot'**

Chapter-36

At the Bookshop
В книжном магазине
(f kneezhnam magazeenye)

An English newspaper, please.

Газету на английском, пожалуйста.

Ga-**zye**-too na an-**gleey**-skam, pa-**zhah**-loos-ta.

I need a map of the area.

Мне нужна карта местности.

Mnye noozh-**nah kahr**-ta **myes**-nas-tee.

Today's paper, please.

Сегодняшнюю газету, пожалуйста.

See-**vod**-neesh-nyoo-yoo ga-**zye**-too, pa-**zhah**-loos-ta.

I am looking for a jokebook in English.

Я ищу книгу анекдотов на английском.

Yah ee-**shchoo knee**-goo a-neeg-**do**-taf na an-**gleey**-skam.

Chapter-37

Small Talk
Светский разговор
(svyetskeey razgavor)

Good morning, sir/madam!
Доброе утро, сэр/мадам!
Dob-ra-ye **oot**-ra, ser/ma-**dahm**!

How are you?
Как дела?
Kak dee-**lah**?

Very well.
Отлично.
At-**leech**-na.

What is your name?
Как вас зовут?
Kak vahs za-**voot**?

My name is...
Меня зовут...
Mee-**nyah** za-**voot**...

Where do you come from?
Откуда вы?
At-**koo**-da vi?

I am from India.
Я из Индии.
Yah eez **Een**-dee-yee.

Do you live there?
Вы там живете?
Vi tahm zhi-**vyo**-tye?

Where are you going?
Куда вы идете?
Koo-**dah** vi ee-**dyo**-tye?

What are you doing?
Что вы делаете?
Shto vi **dye**-la-yee-tye?

What business are you in?
Чем вы занимаетесь?
Chem vi za-nee-**mah**-yee-tyes'?

Do you speak English?

Вы говорите по-английски?

Vi ga-va-**ree**-tye po-an-**gleey**-skee?

I don't understand Russian.

Я не понимаю русский.

Yah nye pa-nee-**mah**-yoo **roos**-keey.

Could you please speak more slowly?

Говорите помедленнее, пожалуйста.

Ga-va-**ree**-tye pa-**myed**-leen-nee-ye, pa-**zhah**-loos-ta.

I can't speak Russian.

Я не говорю по-русски.

Yah nye ga-va-**ryoo** po-**roos**-kee.

I speak a little Russian.

Я немного говорю по-русски.

Yah neem-**no**-ga ga-va-**ryoo** po-**roos**-kee.

Are you married?

Вы женаты/замужем?

Vi zhi-**nah**-ti/**zah**-moo-zhim?

Yes, I'm married.

Да, я женат/замужем.

Dah, yah zhi-**naht/zah**-moozhim.

No, I am not married.

Нет, я не женат/не замужем.

Nyet, yah nye zhi-**naht**/ nye **zah**-moo-zhim.

When is your birthday?

Когда ваш день рождения?

Kag-**dah** vahsh dyen' razh-**dye**-nee-ya?

What is your age?

Сколько вам лет?

Skol'-ka vahm lyet?

I am 25 years old.

Мне 25 лет.

Mnye 25 lyet.

What do you do?

Чем вы занимаетесь?

Chem vi za-nee-**mah**-yee-tyes'?

I am a writer.
Я писатель.
Yah pee-**sah**-tyel'.

Have you come for the first time here?
Вы здесь в первый раз?
Vi zdyes' f **pyer**-viy rahs?

How long do you plan to stay?
Сколько вы планируете здесь пробыть?
Skol'-ka vi pla-**nee**-roo-yee-tye zdyes' pra-**bit'**?

Another week/two weeks.
Еще неделю/две недели.
Yee-**shcho** nee-**dye**-lyoo/dvye nee-**dye**-lee.

It is very nice here.
Здесь очень хорошо.
Zdyes' **o**-cheen' kha-ra-**sho**.

It's been great meeting you.
Рад(а) встречи с вами.
Raht/**rah**-da **vstrye**-chee s **vah**-mee.

Keep in touch.

До встречи.

Do **vstrye**-chi.

With great pleasure.

С удовольствием.

S oo-da-**vol'**-stvee-yem.

Whatever you like

Как хотите

Kak kha-**tee**-tye

Ok (all right)

Окей

O-kyey

I am ok, thanks.

Я в порядке, спасибо.

Yah f pa-**ryaht**-kye, spa-**see**-ba.

It's nice of you to help.

Спасибо за помощь.

Spa-**see**-ba za **po**-mashch.

Were you waiting for me?

Вы меня ждали?

Vi mee-**nyah zhdah**-lee?

I don't like that.

Мне это не нравится.

Mnye **e**-ta nye **nrah**-veet-sya.

No thanks.

Нет, спасибо.

Nyet, spa-**see**-ba.

Wait a moment.

Подождите минуту.

Pa-dazh-**dee**-tye mee-**noo**-too.

It doesn't matter.

Это неважно.

E-ta nee-**vahzh**-na.

Tomorrow is my last day here.

Завтра мой последний день.

Zahf-tra moy pas-**lyed**-neey dyen'.

I am here with my family.
Я здесь с семьей.
Yah zdyes' s seem'-**yoy**.

I would like to introduce you to...
Я хочу представить вас ...
Yah kha-**choo** preet-**stah**-veet' vahs...

This is my child/colleague.
Это мой ребенок/коллега.
E-ta moy ree-**byo**-nak/kal-**lye**-ga.

This is my friend.
Это мой друг.
E-ta moy drook.

This is my wife.
Это моя жена.
E-ta ma-**yah** zhi-**nah**.

This is my husband.
Это мой муж.
E-ta moy moosh.

Chapter-38

Greetings

Приветствия (preevyetstveeya)

All the best!
Всего хорошего!
Fsee-**vo** kha-**ro**-shi-va!

And the same to you!
И тебе тоже!
Ee tee-**bye to**-zhe!

Best wishes!
Всего хорошего!
Fsee-**vo** kha-**ro**-shi-va!

Certainly!
Конечно!
Ka-**nyesh**-na!

Certainly not!
Конечно нет!
Ka-**nyesh**-na nyet!

Congratulations!

Поздравляю!

Paz-drav-**lyah**-yoo!

Excuse me!

Простите!

Pras-**tee**-tye!

Farewell!

Прощай!

Pra-**shchahy**!

Fine

Отлично

At-**leech**-na

Christmas greetings

Рождественские поздравления

Razh-**dyes**-tveen-skee-ye paz-drav-**lye**-nee-ya

Good!

Хорошо!

Kha-ra-**sho**!

Good morning
Доброе утро
Dob-ra-ye **oot**-ra

Good afternoon
Добрый день
Dob-riy dyen'

Good evening
Добрый вечер
Dob-riy **vye**-cheer

Good night
Спокойной ночи
Spa-**koy**-nay **no**-chi

Goodbye
До свидания/ Пока
Do svee-**dah**-nee-ya/ Pa-**kah**

Happy new year!
Счастливого нового года!
Shchas-**lee**-va-va **no**-va-va **go**-da!

Have a good trip!

Хорошей поездки!

Kha-**ro**-shey pa-**yest**-kee!

Hope you have had a lovely time!

Надеюсь, вы хорошо провели время!

Na-**dye**-yoos', vi kha-ra-**sho** pra-vee-**lee vrye**-mya!

How are you?

Как дела?

Kak dee-**lah**?

I am fine

Я хорошо

Yah kha-ra-**sho**

I am pleased to meet you

Рад/рада встречи

Rat/**rah**-da **vstrye**-chi

I see!

Ясно!

Yahs-na!